To my old friend,
former colleague and
fellow writer
Hong An, who
knew Barbara very
well,

Cheers,

Harry Dossett

HARRY GOSSETT

# RINGSIDE to RACISM

## A Love Story

# PREAMBLE

This is not intended to be an accurate history. Neither my wife nor I maintained diaries. Others who were there and witnessed some of these events may remember them differently than I do. Public records may not support my version of all these incidents. However, this is how I recall a few of the myriad adventures I shared with the love of my life.

I can tell you with no fear of contradiction that we had a happier marriage than most. People commented on it regularly. After 49 years together folks still asked us if we were newlyweds. We made one another laugh every day and we never parted company without kissing, saying "I love you," and meaning it.

From my perspective, our relationship was an ongoing conversation. I have stopped talking to her aloud, but I still hear her voice. You can listen in on my memories.

# CHAPTER ONE

# Getting in Love

"Who *is* that woman?"

Pete, an Assistant United States Attorney I had been walking with, noticed that I had stopped abruptly. He saw where I was looking, across the crowded hallway. "Oh. That's Barbara Rowan. She's a new Assistant. Want me to introduce you?"

"Absolutely."

Before that moment, I had difficulty with the notion of "falling in love." That expression makes it seem like a trap you are lured into and cannot escape from. I thought everyone *grew* into love of whatever kind: love of family, love of coffee, love of country, love of music, love of friends, etc. Are we born with an inherent love of dogs? Perhaps, but I was sure we develop an affection for people, places, and things.

I had defined romantic love as a situation where you cannot feel good unless your beloved feels good.

Love at first sight seemed ridiculous.

I vividly remember her eyes. She was near sighted, so her thick glasses made her chocolate brown eyes seem much larger than they were. Her "race" never entered my mind. I was colorblind in that regard, but she did not have that luxury.

My pal Pete introduced us. She was less taken with me than I was with her. Fixated on her eyes, I watched her look me up and down. Later, she told me that the only positive thing she noticed that day was that I was looking at her face. Most males stared at her abundant chest, which she refused to minimize by rounding her shoulders. She stood ramrod straight.

There had to be a way I could get to meet with her, again. It was not long before I found one.

I did an undercover buy from two 70-year-olds at Penn Station. One was on crutches and the other in a wheelchair. They had a few million dollars in stolen U.S. Treasury bills, and I was presented as a dishonest broker who could convert such ill-gotten loot to cash. The case congealed so quickly that I had only one other agent on-scene backing me up. The wheelchair felon tried to get away. I chased him down 33rd Street while my colleague detained the other senior citizen, who could not run because he was on crutches.

We processed the prisoners at the FBI office. Filling in the boxes on the fingerprint card, I asked Mr. Hot Wheels his occupation.

"I'm 70 years old, young man. I am retired."

"What did you retire from?"

He said he had been the editor of a newspaper in Buffalo, New York.

"When did you retire?"

"1928."

"Well, here we are in 1971. How have you been supporting yourself for the past 43 years?"

"I'm not proud of the fact, but I have to admit that women have been taking care of me all these years."

"Women? Wives? Relatives?"

"Girlfriends."

I took the old guys to the U.S. Attorney's office where the head of the Criminal Division would assign an Assistant to prosecute their case. I knew him, so I felt free to suggest that the new Assistant, Miss Rowan, probably didn't have a heavy caseload yet.

He chuckled. "Sounds like you've seen her."

I smirked, too. "I have indeed."

To put this in prospective, in 1970 only 4% of lawyers were women and nearly none of them were trial lawyers. In 1971 the women of Columbia Law School filed a class action lawsuit against ten major New York law firms for discrimination against women applicants in their hiring practices.

Miss Rowan was only the second female AUSA the United States Attorney had placed in the Criminal Division.

I wheeled one defendant into her office and the other swung himself inside. She seemed amused. And she would continue to do so for nearly a half century, much to my delight.

I quickly explained the case, and she asked, "So where did he find you guys? Actors' Equity, or what?" She thought someone was pranking the newest law-yer in the office.

Even the arrestees laughed.

"This is not a practical joke, Miss Rowan. I need a lawyer to represent the United States in their first appearance before a judge."

"I love saying that," she said. "When I introduce myself, I get to add, 'and I represent the United States of America.' I hope that patriotic pride never wears off."

The guy on crutches, a disbarred lawyer who had been a partner in a large law firm, said, "You could make much more money representing private clients."

I thought of several snarky remarks I would have made had I been sitting on her side of the desk, but she simply smiled at the old criminal.

The magistrate did not. He had a courtroom full of defendants and their lawyers waiting for him to set bail in their cases. He insisted we present our man on crutches first.

Miss Rowan explained the charges and the magistrate addressed the offender by his first name. "Do you have anything to say for yourself?"

"You know me. You used to be my law clerk. You know I wouldn't knowingly try to sell stolen treasury bills."

The man behind the bench exploded. "You're damn right I know you! I wouldn't believe you on a stack of bibles to the ceiling!"

A group gasp sucked all the oxygen out of the room. If this was the way he treats his friends, what chance did any of these strangers have for a low bail?

Once our prisoners were turned over to the U.S. Marshals, I walked Miss Rowan back to her office. We agreed this was going to be an interesting case. We thought it was amazing that 70-year-olds were still committing crimes. (When we turned 70, we laughed about how naïve we were in our youth.)

She wanted to see reports right away, and I wanted to see her as often as possible, so we scheduled a meeting.

The following day, I got a call from the woman I had dreamed about all night. "Remember that guy in the wheelchair you arrested yesterday?"

"I don't arrest paraplegics every day."

"You told me he said his girlfriends supported him. Right?"

"Right."

"I had a half dozen of them in my office this morning asking where they could pay his bail."

"At the same time?"

"That was the weird part. They all knew each other. It was like his own private harem, but they were all professional women. They wanted to pool their money and get him out as soon as possible. Each said she loves him and even loves his other women."

"Could you find out what he's doing to keep them all happy?"

"I'm not going to ask intimate questions."

"If you would, I could spread the word among the guys. You and I could bring about peace on earth."

"I'm going to hang up now, Agent Gossett. Have a nice day."

"I am having one already, thanks to you, Miss Rowan."

# CHAPTER TWO
## *Hot Pursuit*

"Here are the theft reports on those treasury bills I recovered."

"Thank you."

The United States Attorney's office was in the federal courthouse just a few blocks north of the Wall Street financial district where I worked. It was convenient for me to stop by and deliver documents to Miss Rowan at her office. I always arrived at the close of business, so at the end of our meeting I could suggest we could go out for a drink, or dinner.

"No thank you." Miss Rowan never made excuses, like other women did. Nothing like, "Oh, I would love to, but tonight I have my violin lesson," or "I promised to babysit my sister's kids," or some other unlikely story.

One day, she was excited to learn from me that both our defendants had recently been released from prison, after having been convicted of selling stolen treasury bills taken in the same theft as the bills I recovered.

I asked, "What is your first name, Miss Rowan?"

"Barbara." She looked puzzled. "Pete told you that when he introduced us."

"The initials on your briefcase, and your pen set, are NBR. Isn't Barbara your middle name?"

"Oh. Those things belonged to my daddy. His name was Norman Barrington Rowan."

I was charmed by the fact this prim and proper beauty referred to her father as her "daddy." How adorable.

The only additional information she shared about him was that he was dead, but she did caution me about her name. "It annoys me that every other Assistant is called 'Mr.' plus his surname. Everyone, even the young women on the support staff, address me as 'Barbara.' I appreciate the fact that you call me 'Miss Rowan.'"

"Yes, ma'am. Miss Rowan."

For younger readers, I should explain that prior to the Women's Movement of the 1960s, females were called "Miss" from birth to marriage and "Mrs." thereafter.

It was a strict protocol. Accidentally addressing a "Miss" as "Mrs." could insult her, if she imagined that you thought she was too long in the tooth to still be unmarried.

And calling a married woman "Miss" might set her off if she took it that her elevated rank was not obvious to one and all.

Mumbling "Mizz" was an effort to be polite when caught in the awkward situation of not knowing a woman's marital status, but you would usually be scolded. "There is no such word as 'Mizz.'"

Women's Lib solved the dilemma by making "Mizz" the preferred form of address. They spelled it "Ms." to conform it with "Mr." (which does not convey a man's marital status).

Many, if not most, women clung to the tradition. Barbara Rowan called herself "Miss Rowan" until the day she died, in 2020. She was also Mrs. Gossett, but most folks didn't know that. Women seeking equal rights back in the day often continued to use their maiden names.

———————

"I hate to cut this short, but I am scheduled to do a presentation this evening."

After politely declining several suggestions for an evening together, Miss Rowan flipped to the other side of the request late one afternoon in her office.

"Oh. Where?"

"Hostos College in the South Bronx. Wanna come?"

"Sure. What is your lecture about?"

"It's not a lecture. Merely a little presentation about job opportunities in the Justice Department. Students in the South Bronx would never think to apply. You could tell them about openings in the FBI."

"No. I couldn't. I would need permission and that would take days."

"Sorry. I thought you might enjoy it."

"If you promise not to tell them I am an FBI agent I'll go."

"How do I explain you?"

"Say I am an employee of the Justice Department. That's true and doesn't involve the magic letters."

———————

What Miss Rowan had failed to tell me about the evening class was that it was taught in Spanish, and she would be doing her presentation in an elegant form of that language, while responding to students who spoke new-world dialects.

She was surprised that evening when I said my few words in Spanish. I told the tired night students that I was a Justice Department employee who was helping Miss Rowan prepare for a trial.

I was surprised to learn that she had lived almost all her life a mile from that classroom, just across the 145th Street Bridge in Harlem. I would have guessed Park Avenue in Midtown.

As we trudged through the snow toward the subway station, we encountered a teenage street gang, armed with a variety of clubs and chains.

"Don't worry," said Miss Rowan. "They are not here for us. They are waiting for another gang. They're gonna rumble."

"How do you know that?"

"That's what they are talking about."

That was my first exposure to Miss Rowan's incredibly keen hearing, and phenomenal language ability.

As we passed, one of the little rascals insulted me, in Spanish, so I stopped, bellied up to the brat, and asked him, in Spanish, to repeat what he had said. He opened his coat to display a .25 automatic in his belt. I opened my coat and showed him my .357 magnum. He gulped audibly. I plucked his pea shooter out of his pants, dropped it in my pocket, and escorted Miss Rowan away, hoping she was favorably impressed.

A few hundred feet later, I said, "Oh, look, there's a coffee shop on the second floor of that building. Want to have a cup and watch the rumble?"

"Yes. And I'd like to know why you didn't tell me you're Puerto Rican."

"Because I'm not. Why would you think so?"

"The way you speak Spanish."

"I went to the University of Puerto Rico. Did you or your parents immigrate from Spain? You speak Spanish Spanish."

"My daddy immigrated from Jamaica and my mother is from Philadelphia. I studied Spanish Language and Literature at the University of Madrid."

We sat down in the coffee shop and continued to chat while watching the street gangs beat on each other, until the police arrived in force and rounded up the herd of juvenile delinquents.

I asked Miss Rowan, "Did they assign this gig to you because you speak Spanish, or did you ask for it since you live nearby?"

"Neither. Ralph, the professor, wanted his students to widen their horizons. He's the reason I am an Assistant United States Attorney."

"He recommended you?"

"No. He got evicted. He and his wife are both professors at Columbia. That's his day job. So, the university provided them housing, until the powers that be decided to tear down their apartment building to construct more classrooms. They were ordered to move out immediately, midterm, with no opportunity to find a place to move their tons of books.

Other lawyers told them they had no recourse, they had to move right away, despite their workload, but they hired me. Since Ralph is an army colonel..."

"What? That frumpy little guy is in the army?"

"You would never recognize the professor when he is in uniform. Very spiffy. He is a reserve officer now, but he has considerable army experience. He's a paratrooper."

"Amazing."

"Anyway, there are federal laws protecting veterans and I found one that applied. After we won, the judge called me aside and asked if I would like to be an Assistant United States Attorney, because he knew the U.S. Attorney was looking for female lawyers. I said I would love a job like that if it meant trial work. I didn't want to spend my time writing appeals or something. The judge said he would recommend me as a trial lawyer because I had impressed him."

"Yeah. You beat the sox off a bigtime law firm representing a major university."

After the police had mopped up the mopes, Miss Rowan would not let me take her to her door. We parted company on the subway train. She said, "I have been walking home from this station late at night for at least a dozen years. Don't worry about me."

---

Later, I had the .25 automatic fired to compare the bullets with bullets from crime scenes, but it had not apparently been used to shoot anyone. At first, all the cartridges in the weapon failed to fire. They were older than the boy I took it from. Fresh ammo worked fine. There was nothing wrong with the weapon, which was not reported stolen.

In those days, the NYPD returned recovered firearms to their rightful owners, or when that was not possible, as proved to be the case with the .25 automatic, they had them melted down to make manhole covers.

---

Miss Rowan invited me to go out with her again. "I'm having dinner with a law school classmate. Would you care to join us?"

"Of course, I would."

We ate at a Chinese restaurant on Canal Street, a short walk from the courthouse.

Miss Rowan's friend, Alice, was a brilliant, petite, trial lawyer from the Legal Aid Society. Her work involved cross-examining police officers and she did something like that throughout dinner. "How would you know that?" "Why would you think that?" "Do you expect us to believe that?"

Specifically, I pointed out a group of men at a table in the back. "Those guys are mafiosi. Little Italy is right across the street." Both women said I was trying to impress them. Which was true, but I wasn't lying.

A year later, those same men met at the same restaurant before they crossed over Canal Street to Little Italy and assassinated Joey Gallo at Umberto's Clam House. By then, neither of my dinner mates remembered seeing them or challenging me.

In those pre-cellphone days, FBI agents who were not at home, or in a Bureau car, were expected to advise the office where they could be reached by phone, or they had to call the switchboard every hour to check for messages. A half century after that clumsy evening, I learned from Alice (now a retired judge) that when I excused myself to do a message

14

check, Miss Rowan had turned to her and said, "So? What do you think?"

"About what?"

"Don't you think he would be right for you?"

"Are you insane? It is obvious that man adores you."

Miss Rowan had told me shortly after dinner with Alice that she was hoping to fix me up with her friend, but it had not worked out.

---

A milestone in our relationship came when Miss Rowan invited me to come to her home in Harlem and meet her mother. At last! I thought she might finally be thinking of me as potential marriage material.

She gave me detailed instructions about which subway train to take and which direction to walk from the station. She was so meticulous that I wondered how hazardous her Harlem neighborhood might be.

Convent Avenue was the opposite of a dangerous place. It was a tree-lined street. The buildings for which it was named had indeed been Catholic convents. Across the street from Miss Rowan's abode was Hamilton Grange, the only mansion Alexander Hamilton ever owned.

(It had been moved a half block in 1889 to accommodate the Manhattan street grid and it would be moved again in 2008 to an open area in St. Nicholas Park.)

I learned that except for her time at the University of Madrid, and a tour of Europe, Miss Rowan had lived in a large first-floor apartment at 310 Convent Avenue with her mom, dad, and grandmother.

I knew her father and her grandmother were deceased. Her mother, Clara, was the nicest person I ever met. She lived with us for the last ten years of her life and my opinion never changed. She was of a lighter complexion than her daughter, so she was often taken to be a White person. Living her entire life on the color line, she felt it was her duty to explain members of one race to members of the other. That embarrassed her daughter.

Miss Rowan and I were side by side on a sofa facing Mrs. Rowan who was sitting in a chair telling me about the Harlem Renaissance. Her daughter kept trying to change the subject and started to sound quite rude, so I pulled a hillbilly stunt. I grew up on the edge of the Ozark Mountains. "Excuse me, ma'am. Do you mind if I spank your daughter?"

Miss Rowan's jaw dropped. Her mother smiled happily. "I don't think Barbara has ever been spanked. It would do her a world of good." Our sub-ject gasped aloud.

I put her across my lap and gave the seat of her snug pedal pushers a few swats. Clara giggled. When I sat Miss Rowan back up, she said, "That hurt!" With her arms crossed, she stuck out her lower lip, and glared at me.

I turned back to her mother, and we continued our pleasant conversation about the Harlem Renaissance without further interruption. Miss Rowan pouted and snorted, much to her mother's delight.

My flawed legal theory was that, despite her age, a woman who still lives at home is an unemancipated adult child. Thus, a spanking authorized by one of her parents was not an Assault and Battery, as it otherwise would be, but rather a parental punishment carried out by an assistant.

A major problem with my position had to do with who paid the bills. I might have been on better ground had Miss Rowan been living off her mother's largess, but when Mr. Rowan died, his daughter became the sole support for both her mother who (I would later learn) was legally blind and crippled, and her grandmother, who was suffering from dementia.

In any event, I faked a lighthearted conversation with Mrs. Rowan while my conscience screamed at me: *"YOU IDIOT! You met the most beautiful woman in the world. You cajoled her to bring you into her home and meet her mother. And what did you do? YOU SPANKED HER! Right in front of her mother! Who she lives with! Sees every day! Her mom will probably tell all their friends and relatives, and the neighbors. Miss Rowan will never live it down! She will never forgive you! She will get your case reassigned so she will never have to see you face to face again! YOU FOOL!"*

I finally checked my watch. "Well, I have to be going." I felt I was walking out of her life forever. My stomach was in a knot.

Miss Rowan popped up, gripped my elbow, and walked me to the door. She didn't stop there. She marched me to the front door of the building and as I stepped down the three steps to the sidewalk, she turned me around, took my head in her hands and gave me a fabulous kiss. We had never kissed before. Without a word, she spun around and went back inside, leaving me totally confused.

*Was that her classy way of kissing me off? Was she letting me know what I would not be getting from her in the future? Or was she showing me she could forgive my manual assault on her hindquarters, but she didn't want her mother to know? Maybe she was thanking me for making her behave.*

I worried about my situation for several days, and sleepless nights. Miss Rowan was a very smart lawyer. What legal recourse did she have? What administrative remedies did the Department of Justice offer? I could hardly wait to see her again. If, in fact, she would see me.

She called me! "Our disbarred lawyer defendant has pled guilty and is scheduled to be sentenced." Her tone was the same calm, precise, timber I was accustomed to, and loved.

She said, "I don't know the protocol. Do FBI agents normally go to sentencings?"

"Not necessarily, but I have gone to sentencings, and I would like to be there for this one."

She gave me the time and date and suggested that I come to her office first. We could go to the courtroom together.

Yay! All was not lost. She had not mentioned my boorish behavior in her living room. She had invited me to be with her. Who could ask for anything more?

---

The sentencing proved entertaining for Miss Rowan and me, but for no one else in the courtroom, except perhaps the judge.

At the appointed time for the sentencing, a complicated civil matter was being argued before him by two Wall Street lawyers in pinstripe suits. He asked the one at the podium to stop while he sentenced a man in a criminal matter.

The looks on the faces of the expensive litigators indicated neither of them had ever seen a sentencing before.

And it got more entertaining when the old man on crutches was ushered in.

The judge asked if the defendant had anything to say.

"As you know, your honor, I was once a partner in a New York law firm, so I have no excuse for my crime. However, I would like for you to postpone my sentencing because I have not yet told my 92-year-old mother that I have been arrested."

"Have your lawyer tell her."

The two best dressed individuals in the courtroom were staring at one another with their mouths hanging open.

The judge sentenced the disbarred lawyer to several years in prison.

The defendant collapsed.

His honor waved his hand at him and told the marshals to "get this out of here."

They carried the man and his crutches away.

The panting litigator at the podium could not get a sentence together when the judge told him to "go on."

Moments later, Miss Rowan and I shared a hearty laugh in the hallway.

---

On another day, after I had testified in court, I ran into Miss Rowan in the hall. Both our cases had resulted in convictions. While we were chatting, one of her jurors said in passing, "Your parents must be so proud of you."

Miss Rowan smiled politely, but when the jury member was out of earshot, she snorted. "She wouldn't have said that if I were a White male."

"Why would you think that?"

"After all they invested in my education, my parents expected me to have a professional career. I'm only doing what was expected of me."

I said, "My family merely hoped I would get a job."

"The doctors in my family are considered more successful than the lawyers."

"Perhaps you should have become a doctor."

"I planned to. When I was fifteen, I volunteered at Mount Sinai Hospital as a Spanish interpreter. I got a white coat and a stethoscope, so most people there thought I was a doctor. I looked older than I was."

"What made you change your mind?"

"For one thing, my job was very upsetting. The doctors seem to think that Spanish speaking women were overly dramatic about their pain. It wasn't long before I would translate 'This will sting a little' to '*Esto ardará como el infierno*' (This will burn like hell)."

"At least you gave them fair warning."

"I did. And when the doctors asked, 'How bad is the pain, on a scale of one to ten,' I would always say 'ten' no matter what the patient said in Spanish, because I wanted her to get some pain meds."

"I can see why you didn't want to practice medicine."

"The clencher was the cafeteria. My grandmother was a chef. She would have thrown out most of the slop doctors eat at the hospital. The first time I was taken to dinner at a fine restaurant, by a lawyer, I said to myself, 'I want to be a lawyer.'"

# CHAPTER THREE
## *Dating*

"What are you doing out here?" I could hear her teeth chattering.

"You were supposed to meet me an hour ago!"

"I was sitting at the bar waiting for you."

"You were inside getting drunk while I was freezing in the snow?"

"I'm not drunk."

"You smell like Jack Daniels."

What an extraordinary sense of smell she had. She had identified the brand of bourbon I had been drinking.

I said, "Through the window, I could see your hat with snow piling up on it, but I thought it was a mailbox."

"This is New York City we don't have outside mailboxes."

"I'm so sorry."

"Why would you think I would go into a bar looking for a man?"

"That's where everyone else meets. Please come inside."

"Every bus that stopped right in front of me would have taken me home."

"Please come in, have a hot meal, and tell me about the buses."

"Well, okay. I need to warm up and maybe I can tempt you to ride on a bus now and then. Even though subway trains are faster, you can see the life of the city from a bus. I do a lot of window-shopping that way. I can look over the tops of the parked cars and pedestrians. You can't see much from a taxi."

———————

"What a clever idea." I had slipped up behind Miss Rowan in a crowd.

"What idea?" She had recognized my voice before she turned around.

"Telling me to meet you at the clock."

"As you can see, lots of people meet at the clock here in Grand Central Station. With thousands of people per minute going through this enormous lobby, how else could we find each other?"

"I have to tell you I picked you out before you got to the clock."

"How?"

"The way you walk. You are the most graceful person in this throng."

"I guess all those years of ballet helped."

"You were a ballet dancer?"

"Till I broke my ankle."

"A bad landing from a jump?"

"No. A crack in the sidewalk. I was roller skating."

For the next fifty years I would find out interesting facts about Miss Rowan's past in conversations like this. She never bragged about her accomplishments, complained about failures, or volunteered information. But she always answered my questions, and she was honest to a fault.

It worked both ways. She was often surprised to learn of something I had done in my youth which was news to her.

In the 21st century we watched the television quiz show Jeopardy together. Hardly an evening went by without one or both of us asking, "How in the world did you know that?" If we could recall where we gained that knowledge, it often led to revelations about our lives.

---

"Harry, you probably have other plans for tomorrow night, but I have two tickets to…"

"Yes. I would love to go."

"I haven't told you what the tickets are for."

"You have taken me to Carnegie Hall, The Lincoln Center, and a Broadway play. I know it will be something good."

"I know you date other women …"

"I have only taken you to the movies and dinners. That's because I lack your familiarity with cultural events."

"Have you read The French Connection? They made a movie out of it."

"No. I never read that book. But I know the author. I'll take you to the movie."

"You know Robin Moore?"

"Yeah. I have had a few drinks with him at P.J. Clark's. He's a nice guy."

"P.J. Clark's huh? I have heard you did your bar hopping on the singles strip."

"Who told you that?"

"You are not the only FBI agent I work with."

"Their information is out of date. The young women in the singles bars are geographically undesirable."

"Oh?"

"Yeah. They come in from Connecticut, Long Island, Pennsylvania, all over. Dating is impossible."

"Dating? I didn't know hooking up on First Avenue had anything to do with dating."

"There is more to life than one-night stands."

---

"Would you mind checking my math?" She tossed her personal checkbook across her desk to me.

I was stunned! Miss Rowan had never volunteered information about herself.

Younger readers, please understand that in those days credit cards had not yet taken over. Everything was paid for by cash or check. Miss Rowan was giving me access to the record of her spending.

Privacy was more important back then as well.

While she was reviewing legal papers, I scanned the numbers column in her checkbook. I was shocked! Maybe she was testing me. Whoever added and subtracted those numbers could not do simple arithmetic.

"Did you do this?"

"Yes. I am not good with numbers. That's why I asked you to check it and correct my mistakes."

"Right here," I pointed out one error, "you added three and three and got five."

"What should I have gotten?"

"Six."

"My daddy's accounting firm hired me right out of college. I only lasted two weeks. He fired me when he found out I couldn't do basic math."

"You lasted two weeks?"

"They had a big adding machine. You know, one of those things with a handle on the side. I could input numbers and pull the handle."

"That's what you need, a calculator. They make little battery powered ones you can keep in your purse."

For the next half century, I marveled at how a woman so brilliant in so many ways could not deal with numbers.

Without her little calculator, she could never have passed her flight exam. Fortunately, they had just started to allow the use of calculators during the test.

The week before she came down with Covid-19, which took her life, she turned to me one morning at the breakfast table and asked, "What's forty divided by four?" She wasn't kidding.

---

"What have we here?" Miss Rowan eyed the motorcycle in my living room.

"That belongs to Steve. He's an FBI agent I share the apartment with.

"Don't let the landlord catch you with a motor vehicle in the apartment."

"They already did. But that Norton Commando is not licensed in the United States. See, it still has a British tag. So, we argued that it is a telephone chair."

She laughed. "I can't believe they bought that."

"The jury is still out."

"Too bad we can't ride it."

"I'm not licensed to ride a bike in New York."

"Wouldn't you love to learn?"

"I didn't say I don't know how. My dad sold Harley Davidsons."

"Do you think Steve would mind if I sat on it?"

"It is just a telephone chair. Go ahead."

"Ooops!"

That was the first but certainly not the last time I saw Miss Rowan fall off a motorcycle. Each crash frightened me more as we aged. She hit the pavement harder and harder. Miraculously, she never broke a bone, and it never broke her spirit.

# CHAPTER FOUR
## *Our First Trip*

"Do you have plans for Thanksgiving?" Miss Rowan asked.

"No. Do you have plans for me?"

"Maybe. My Uncle Charlie and Aunt Elaine have invited us to join them. Wanna come?"

"Count me in."

"They live in Philadelphia. I'll rent a car."

"Let me do that."

"Okay."

I had learned that renting a parking space in New York City was more expensive than renting my studio apartment in Miami had been. No one needed a personally owned vehicle in Manhattan. Walking, or riding on buses, the subway, or in taxis was far more practical. In fact, 70% of the residents did not have driver's licenses.

---

"Let me walk you to the car." Miss Rowan had told me about her mother's limitations. I had been skeptical. Clara supported herself so subtly on her furniture as she walked around her apartment, her eyes moved, and she looked at the things she talked about.

It was only when I walked her outside that I understood how blind and unbalanced she was. She gripped my arm like a koala clutches a Eucalyptus and she had to feel around to find the open car door.

---

"Perhaps I should have let you drive, Barbara." I started calling her "Barbara" on that trip.

"Don't get huffy because I'm giving you directions. I've driven this route many times."

"I appreciate your expert navigation, but I don't think it's necessary for you to tell me which lane to drive in, or how fast to go."

"You drive slower than my granddaddy. And he's dead."

I turned to the back seat passenger. "What do you think, Clara? Would you like me to drive faster? I can certainly do that."

"I'm sorry. I wasn't listening."

I thought she was politely lying to stay out of our disagreement, but in fact Barbara's mother had tuned us out. She did that a lot over the next decade. Not that we argued a lot. We had to tell Clara what we were talking about to elicit an opinion from her. She ignored our conversations so as not to intrude.

"Okay, ladies. Tighten your seatbelts."

"Now don't do anything stupid, Harry." Barbara started calling me "Harry" on that trip, too.

Night had fallen as we neared our destination. The narrow road alongside the winding Wissahickon Creek was a thrill a minute. The locals made a first timer like me feel he had accidentally driven into a Formula One race, on a slick road in the dark at freezing temperatures.

I was up to it, and my passengers were used to it.

My adorable navigator vectored me through Germantown, onto Ardleigh Street, and ultimately down a paved alley, with a park on the right and garages on the left. "See the marked parking space? Park there."

Barbara collected Clara and I toted the luggage toward a gate in a chain link fence with a light over it.

"Oh, there's Fritz," said Barbara cheerfully.

I expected a relative to emerge into the light, but no, a vicious German Shepard leaped out of the dark toward my face in full attack mode. Fortunately, he was chained but his open mouth came close enough for me to smell his breath and count his teeth.

"Cha Cha, come get Fritz," Barbara called out.

Uncle Charlie appeared and ordered his dog to settle down. Fritz loped away dragging a long heavy chain.

When we entered the house, Barbara said, "That stew needs more salt."

I asked, "How could you know that?"

"Can't you smell it?"

That was how I learned of her extraordinary sense of smell.

Aunt Elaine asked, "What are your intentions toward my niece?"

We had yet to be introduced.

I gestured toward Barbara. "I'll refer you to my legal counsel."

"No, you won't. I have a conflict of interest. I'll be in the kitchen doctoring the stew. You're on your own, big boy."

I waited until I thought she was out of earshot. "I plan to spend as much time with your niece as is humanly possible."

"Harrumph."

---

"Wake up, Harry. Breakfast is ready."

I had slept on the sofa in the living room. Barbara and Clara had shared the guest bedroom.

"Oh. Hi, Barbara. How long have you been up?"

"Long enough. Do you eat scrapple?"

"What is it?"

"We are in Philly, honey. The Pennsylvania Dutch call it Pannhaas."

Call it whatever you like, the scrapple and eggs were delicious.

---

After a hearty breakfast, we left Clara to visit with her brother and sister-in-law while we took a walk to get out of the overheated house.

"This big park is Awbury Arboretum." Barbara waved her hand at the green oasis across the alley.

"How about those old stone houses? Somebody lives there. They have cars parked beside them."

"This was an enclave of an extended Quaker family, back in the day. They donated it to the city about fifty years ago. I'll introduce you to a Quaker couple who live in that one."

"Interesting architecture. The houses don't match."

"Good eyes, Mr. Gossett. That one is Gothic Revival. That one is Queen Anne. And the one over there is Tudor Revival."

"You know more about structural design than I do."

"Probably not. I learned all that from the Quakers who live here."

It turned out they were not at home. I would meet them on our next visit.

We had not brought gloves, so we held hands to keep our fingers warm. That became our lifelong habit. Nearly 50 years later, people still asked us if we were newlyweds when they saw us walking hand in hand.

Barbara liked to say, "No. We are just holding each other up."

On that Thanksgiving morning, we walked across the arboretum to a small commuter rail station. It had a little parking lot. No cars were there. It proved a perfect place to get out of the chilly wind and hug for warmth.

"So, what do you think of my aunt and uncle?"

"She certainly didn't tiptoe around asking me to state my plans for us."

"That's because of her job."

"Is she a marriage counselor? Or a divorce lawyer?"

"No. She works for the Immigration and Naturalization Service."

"What does she do at the INS?"

(On March 1, 2003, the INS was eliminated. Most INS functions were transferred to three agencies at the newly created Department of Homeland Security.)

"Among other things, she interviews people who claim immigration status by virtue of being married to an American citizen. That means she must ask them if they have consummated their marriages."

"So, they can't just be married in name only?"

"Exactly. If she is suspicious, she can ask them separately about their first conjugal event. When and where they did it. What their spouse's genitals look like. Stuff like that. She has a hard bark on her."

"I guess they have to answer, if they want to enter the country."

"Right. She told me one elderly couple said, 'We tried our best,' but she declined to approve. A week or so later, they called her from a foreign hotel to announce: 'We did it!' So, she invited them to come back."

---

Back at the house, we enjoyed a traditional Thanksgiving dinner: roast turkey, stuffing, mashed potatoes, gravy, green beans, corn, dinner rolls, cranberry sauce, and pumpkin pie.

"Did Barbara tell you that Muhammad Ali used to live right next door?" Aunt Elaine asked.

"No, she didn't. I had dinner with him a couple of years ago."

"You and a hundred other people."

"No. Just me, my date, and Muhammad Ali. He had been doing a Broadway show, you know, after they stripped him of his title because he refused to be drafted. They had denied his application to serve as a noncombatant."

Elaine's face radiated skepticism.

"Harry doesn't lie," said Barbara.

"Oh." Elaine relaxed noticeably.

I went on. "It was after the FBI Christmas dance two years ago. I took my date across the street to the Stage Deli, and they gave us a table for two. Then the maître d' came back and said, 'We are all out of tables. Do you mind if we put another chair at your table?' We said we wouldn't mind. That other person turned out to be Muhammed Ali. He was very friendly and chatty. Nicest guy in the room."

Barbara asked, "What did you talk about?"

"We didn't talk about boxing, or Broadway, or the FBI. We shared Christmas stories and ate those enormous Stage Deli sandwiches."

"What happened to that girlfriend?" asked Elaine.

"She wasn't Barbara."

# CHAPTER FIVE
## *A Night to Remember*

"Hope I haven't made you late for your dinner date, Harry."

The new Chief of Security at the Federal Reserve Bank, a recently retired FBI agent, was giving me an afterhours tour. He knew me and my assignment, so he wanted to show me how the Fed processed treasury securities.

"Her office is nearby," I said. "She's an Assistant U.S. Attorney."

At that point, one of his subordinates rushed up to us. "Sir. I need to talk to you…" The man eyeballed me, indicating he needed a private moment with his boss, who asked, "What is it?"

"It's about that million-dollar bill we took in yesterday." He flicked his eyes in my direction, again.

My host said, "It's okay. Harry's an FBI agent. He investigates thefts of treasury bills."

"We were reviewing the films and one of the girls in the office recognized the girl who brought it in. She even knows where the girl lives!"

"Where's that?"

"Bed-Stuy."

From the Security Chief's office, I called my supervisor. He didn't answer his phone. No doubt he was on his way home, or out to dinner, or something.

No one answered any of the phones in our squad room.

I called the night duty supervisor and told him I needed another agent and a car to go interview a woman who redeemed a stolen million-dollar treasury bill.

"Where is she?"

"Bedford–Stuyvesant."

"Bed-Stuy! The cops only go there in force. It's after dark, Harry. You're not taking another agent and a bureau car in there."

"With a million dollars in hand, she's not going to be there long."

"Get your supervisor to hit it with the entire squad at dawn, before the natives get restless."

My retired colleague watched my frustration growing while I was dialing for assistance on his phone. He said, "I don't have any security officers available right now, Harry, but I do have a limousine with an armed driver."

"Good idea."

My next call was to Assistant United States Attorney Barbara Ann Rowan.

---

I got out of the limo so that Barbara could see me in the bright lights that lit up the front of what is now named the Thurgood Marshall United States Courthouse. She floated down the wide granite stairs with all the grace of an angel descending from heaven … in a hurry.

I opened the door of the limo for her.

"Wow! You FBI guys certainly do things in style."

––––––––––

In Bed-Stuy, half the streetlights were not working but the limo still turned heads.

"I'm a retired cop," said our driver. "I worked in the 79th Precinct back in the 60s. The Black population here used to riot against us all the time. It's not that bad now."

"If the limo comes under attack while we are in the building, feel free to leave us and call for police support once you are safely out of danger," I said.

"Don't you kids worry. The NYPD will get you out of here."

Miss Rowan seemed amused by the back and forth between two White men entering a predominately Black neighborhood at midnight.

"Have you been to Bedford–Stuyvesant before?" I asked her.

"Not that I recall."

"Okay, here's the building," said the driver. "The broad you're looking for lives in Apartment 3-A."

We crunched across shards of glass on the sidewalk and found the front door ajar. Both flights of stairs were littered with toys, mostly broken.

A young woman answered her door in her flimsy nightgown.

"Hi. I'm Harry Gossett. I'm an FBI agent…" I held up my credentials.

**Brrriiing!** A telephone rang behind her.

"Come in, come in," she said waving her hand as she rushed to answer the phone.

Miss Rowan jerked her head toward the open door, as though I hadn't understood the invitation. We walked in, and I locked the door. I was more concerned about an attacker entering than a potential rescue party being barred. The latter would probably bring breaching tools.

Miss Rowan's bright eyes followed my every move.

"Now don't you be calling me after midnight," the young woman told someone on the phone. "I just got the baby to sleep, and I got company." She hung up and gestured toward the couch. "Please sit down."

We did so and the nearly naked young mother snuggled between us, facing me. "What you want to know?"

Miss Rowan and I had agreed that, if the woman was willing to be interviewed, whichever one of us she talked to would conduct the questioning.

"First, let me confirm your identity."

"What do you mean?"

I said her name. "That's you, right?"

"Yes, sir."

I took an FBI form captioned "Advice of Rights" out of my inside coat pocket and held it so she could read it. "This is an official FBI interview, so it is important that you know what your rights are. See, the first one here says, 'You have a right to remain silent.' That means you do not have to talk to me. I won't get mad at you if you don't. I get paid the same whether you talk to me or not..."

**Brrriiing!** The phone rang, again.

"I gotta take that before it wakes the baby." She hopped up and flew to the phone.

"Hi ... No, I don't know where he is. ... You're his mother. I'm just his sister. He doesn't tell me... Yes, I did talk to him today, but he didn't say where he planned to be tonight. ... Okay, I will. Please don't call back. The baby's sleeping."

She came back and plunked down between us, again. "Sorry. That was my mom."

"Well, let's get back to your rights. Remember this first one, 'You have a right to remain silent.' That's not an all or nothing deal. You might want to answer some of my questions but not others. In that case you could say, 'I don't want to answer that question,' and I will move on to the next one."

I could see Miss Rowan was wrinkling her brow and I wondered if she disagreed with my opinion.

A loud hiss from the kitchen summoned. "Oh, no!" The young mother ran into the steam filled room.

Miss Rowan leaned close and said, "Why don't you just hand her the form, have her sign it, and get on with the interview?"

"Because I don't want her to go to prison and lose custody of her child."

"Neither do I."

"I want her to get probation because of her cooperation."

"Me too."

"She's not going to cooperate if she doesn't trust me, and she's not going to trust me unless she feels I am concerned about her. Which I am. Watch and learn."

"Humm."

Between cleaning the kitchen, shushing the baby, taking phone calls, and diapering her child, with my help, the woman listened to my efforts to educate her about those rights the Supreme Court ruled that everyone arrested or about to be arrested should be informed of, in the case called *Miranda vs. Arizona.*

Apprising the woman my way took about 45 minutes. Several times I noticed Miss Rowan rolling her eyes behind the young mother's back.

At last, I asked if she would like to sign the form. Our potential defendant said, "Sure," and signed. Miss Rowan scribbled her name as a witness.

I started asking substantive questions and received full cooperation. The ghetto resident gave me everything she knew about the stolen million-dollar-bill that she had cashed.

On the limo ride back to Manhattan, Miss Rowan said, "When you kept dwelling on her rights, I thought you were toying with her. But you were right. That woman would trust you with her life."

"She just did. Now it's our job to make sure the guys she gave up tell us who they were working for. We will worm our way back up the daisy chain so her cooperation will yield greater and greater results."

"If she comes in to plead guilty, like she said she would, I'm sure my office will recommend probation."

"Since you have invested so much time in this case, will they assign it to you?"

"Not a chance. Tonight, I made myself a witness. I can't cross examine myself. But I will stay in touch with whoever gets this case. At least until her plea is adjudicated."

"Good."

---

"Did you get in trouble for taking me with you last night?"

"Not yet. My supervisor is helping me cover that up. Since you didn't use your title or even put "Esq." after your name when you witnessed the rights form, I am only in violation of the rule against a lone agent interviewing a female, particularly in the middle of the night."

(There were no female FBI agents in the New York Office at that time.)

"I see."

"Did you catch any flack?"

"A little. My boss pointed out that although the treasury bill was stolen and redeemed in Manhattan, in the Southern District, we interviewed the suspect in Brooklyn, that's in the Eastern District. I am not an Assistant U.S. Attorney on that side of the river. The U.S. Attorney over there might raise a ruckus if he finds out I was poaching in his district."

---

I am happy to report here that the financially desperate young mother pled guilty and got probation. No harm came to her. The two guys who had forced her to cash in the treasury bill also cooperated. They both pled guilty and received reduced prison terms. Four layers of felons implicated whoever they could honestly incriminate, to get shorter sentences.

# CHAPTER SIX
## Love and Marriage

"I don't want to destroy your career," Barbara said, each time I proposed to her.

"If being married to you costs me my job, then the position isn't worth having. Don't worry. You can support me."

"Until the United States Supreme Court decision in *Loving versus Virginia*, just four years ago, interracial marriage was a crime in sixteen southern states. Mildred Loving looks whiter than I do, but they still put her in jail."

"But they can't do that anymore. I read that there are over a hundred interracial married couples in the United States now."

(That was 1971. In 2015 over 16% of U.S. marriages were interracial.)

Finally, Barbara relented, a little. "Why don't we live together for a while and see if we can survive the public pressure?"

"Great idea!" I didn't care if we were married or not. I just wanted to be with Barbara.

I rented a newly refurbished three-room apartment on East 84th Street, only after the landlord told me that he and his wife would make my non-White mate feel welcome. They lived in the building so their assurance eased my concern.

Then I was hit with a stroke of good luck.

"I'm sorry, Harry. I know I said I would live with you, but I can't do this to my mother. She would be totally humiliated if her daughter was living with a man she wasn't married to."

"So, you *will* marry me!"

"I guess I have to. But you will still be stuck with this apartment lease if it doesn't work out."

"Why wouldn't it work out?"

"You don't know how evil people can be to mixed race families. One of my childhood friends married a White guy. She is an actress in Broadway plays and Hollywood movies. When they haul their stuff back and forth, they drive through Canada, rather than the United States."

"Let me deal with the rednecks."

"I was thinking of some of the Black people I know."

"You can deal with them."

"I can. Don't you get involved with any of that."

"Okay."

"Just one more thing. I would like to get married on my parents' anniversary."

"Sure. When's that?"

"January 19th."

The following day, December 22, 1971, I submitted the required form advising FBI Headquarters that I was going to get married on January 19, 1972.

---

"Would it be okay if we got married at a judge's house, rather than a church?"

"I would prefer that, Barbara. Weddings are for the brides, so if you wanted a big church wedding, that would be fine with me. If you want a quiet little wedding, that's even better."

"I worked as an interpreter in Judge Polier's court. She recommended me to NYU Law School, and she has offered to marry us in her house after work."

I would later learn that Justine Wise Polier was the first woman judge in New York State, having been appointed by Mayor Fiorello La Guardia in 1935.

"Did you accept her offer?"

"Contingent on your approval."

"Approved! I would marry you in Macy's front window!"

"I'm planning to only invite my mother, and Alice, and Elliot. Who do you want to bring?"

Alice and Elliot were classmates from NYU Law School. Barbara had shared office space with

Elliot in Greenwich Village before she joined the U.S. Attorney's Office.

"How about my partner, George, and his wife? He could be my best man."

"Fine with me."

---

"Judge Polier?"

"You must be Mr. Gossett. Everyone else is here."

She led me to her parlor where George and his wife were chatting with Barbara's mother, Clara, who they had chauffeured to the event. Alice and Elliot were in on the conversation, too.

The most important person, the bride, was not there.

Our hostess waved her hand in my direction and, in her quiet aristocratic tone, announced, "At last, a man who can tame Barbara Rowan."

I wondered if Barbara or Clara had told her about the spanking I gave Barbara, or if she simply thought of my wife-to-be as a frisky female who needed to be taken in hand.

There were two pleasant surprises for me, and later for Barbara. Elliot had rented a Honeymoon Suite at The Plaza Hotel for us, and Alice had reserved tables at the Oak Room for our reception.

That was extraordinary. For decades, The Plaza Hotel had the open, airy, Palm Court for the ladies. No men allowed. And the dark basement Oak Room for the gentlemen. No women allowed.

The federal court had ruled only a day or two before our wedding that the gender segregation in those two spaces at The Plaza Hotel was unconstitutional.

We milled around Judge Polier's parlor for a long time. Barbara did not show up. Finally, we all agreed that she must have changed her mind.

As we descended the front steps, a taxi screeched to a halt and the bride bounced out.

"Sorry I'm late. You can thank this gentleman, Harry," she indicated the cab driver. "I gave him the choice between bringing me here to be married or taking me to the airport to flee."

The driver acknowledged her statement.

"If all of you come back inside," Judge Polier said graciously, "we can wed this couple."

———————

"This place is as spooky as that night in Bed-Stuy," said Barbara, after we were seated in the Oak Room.

"Your night in Bed-Stuy?" Alice wanted to know all about it.

The dark wood paneling and low light level made it difficult to see all the cigar smoke that the masculine power brokers were pumping into the air. Bass voices muttered all around us each time they heard our ladies' soprano chatter echoing off the vaulted ceiling.

Elliot said, rhetorically, "Aren't we a high-class bunch of civil rights demonstrators?"

The social atmosphere improved minute by minute. A couple of hours after we had invaded the man cave, the cigar smokers were laughing along with us and wishing us well.

––––––––

"What a lovely suite," Barbara said, after I carried her over the threshold.

I said, "These windows would be a perfect place to watch a parade."

Parades in New York City often march north on Fifth Avenue, right past the Plaza Hotel.

Our experience in the Honeymoon Suite got surreal in the middle of the night.

We had assumed we were in a king size bed, which appeared to be the case. However, when we were both in the center of it, the two single beds drifted apart and we fell to the floor between them, with a loud *THUMP!*

*"Ack!"* said Barbara.

"Are you alright?"

"I can't breathe. An elephant fell on me."

"Before I try to move you, I need to know if we broke any of your bones."

"I don't know. But please help me up. The floor is cold."

Thus, we spent our wedding night cuddled closely together in a single bed. But that was a good thing. We never wanted to sleep any other way.

Although over the years there were a few exceptional times when physical afflictions forced us to keep our distance, we slept like spoons in a drawer for the vast majority of the next 17,801 nights.

---

Room Service delivered our breakfast and Barbara told me why she was so late to our wedding.

"The jury was out all afternoon. I knew if I told the judge that I was getting married he would send the jury home early and have them come back today. I didn't want them to lose their focus on the facts."

"So, you never told him."

"Yes, I did. After the jury came back with a guilty verdict and he dismissed them. I told him why I had been so restless. My anxiety had nothing to do with the jury's finding, merely the amount of time they were taking."

"Was he surprised?"

"He was angry."

"Why?"

"He was afraid I had lost you … Well, he was also annoyed that I didn't ask him to marry us."

"Really?"

"Yes. He said, 'I could have married you while the jury was out. I have married Blacks and Whites and Filipinos, all sorts of people. You didn't have to go to some other judge.'"

"Blacks and Whites and Filipinos?"

"Those were his exact words. I explained my long relationship with Judge Polier and he seemed to feel a little better. It is not like I know the man, other than appearing in his court a few times."

"Did you really ask the cab driver to choose your future marital status?"

"I did."

"What did he say?"

"He said he and his wife had been happily married for twenty years and I should at least give it a try."

# CHAPTER SEVEN
## *Immediate Reactions*

"That's it? You guys aren't gonna shake hands, or hug, or cry, or anything?"

Barbara was amazed by the single, calm, simultaneous, nods with which my apartment mate and I said our farewells.

Her concern made my taciturn colleague laugh.

She said, "You two have shared this place for years."

"We'll see each other at work."

I gave a hug to my new wife, rather than my old housemate.

---

"You know my unit supervisor, Andy, right?" Barbara asked with a mirthful smirk.

"I've met him. We're not pals."

"He called me into his office today and said he was going to miss me."

"What!"

"I was shocked, too. 'Am I being transferred out of the narcotics unit?' I asked. 'Too late for that,' he said."

"Good grief!"

"So, I asked him, 'Are you firing me?'

'No,' he said, 'I heard you got married."

'And?'

'Don't you plan to quit?'

'No.'

'But you're a married woman now.'

'You're a married man.'

'Don't you plan to have babies?'

'Don't you have a house-load of kids?'

'I guess I should congratulate you, huh?'

'That would be nice.'

I didn't tell him that we don't plan to have kids."

Female lawyers today stand on the shoulders of trailblazers like my wife.

---

While other agents I worked with had received congratulatory letters from J. Edgar Hoover when they married, I received a letter of censure.

OFFICE OF THE DIRECTOR

UNITED STATES DEPARTMENT OF JUSTICE

FEDERAL BUREAU OF INVESTIGATION

WASHINGTON, D.C. 20535

February 7, 1972

PERSONAL

Mr. Harold W. Gossett II
Federal Bureau of Investigation
New York, New York

Dear Mr. Gossett:

In connection with a proposed change in your personal status there was a failure on your part to insure that necessary information pertinent to such matters was furnished to the Bureau in accordance with existing regulations. Your explanation has been considered; however, it is apparent that in this instance you failed to discharge your responsibilities as an employee of the FBI, and you were definitely at fault.

Hereafter, it will be incumbent upon you to display a higher regard for rules and regulations so there will be no basis for similar criticism.

Very truly yours,

John Edgar Hoover
Director

"I knew this would happen." Barbara shook her head. "Hoover won't fire you outright. Your career will bleed to death from daily administrative cuts like this."

"Don't jump to conclusions. I'm proud of this letter. I'm going to frame it."

"What?"

"I have never had a letter of censure before. And what better reason for reprimand could I have wanted? I didn't cause harm or injury. I didn't put anyone in danger. I didn't wreck an investigation. I should '…display a higher regard for rules and regulations…' How cool is that!"

"You are incorrigible."

"Let me explain what happened. I was running out to an undercover meeting. My subject was flying in from Miami and if he didn't see me at the airport with a red scarf around my neck he would simply turn around and fly away. Some headquarters hump called to complain that I had not submitted the form—declaring that I planned to marry you—30 days before our wedding. I said, 'You caught me at a bad time. I'm running out the door. My wife is an Assistant United States Attorney. We investigated her background for that job. She wanted to get married on her mother and father's anniversary date, so I submitted the form the day she said yes. That was 29 days before the ceremony. Okay?'

"He said, 'You don't understand the process. We have to….'

"I said, 'You don't understand. I have to go now.' And I hung up on him.

She said, "I'm not surprised."

"When I got back to the office, there was a tele-type demanding a written explanation for my delin-quency in form-fill-out-ery, so I wrote a memo telling them the same thing I said on the phone. But in a more polite tone."

"So?"

"This admonishment is for my bad attitude. If I had taken the time to grovel, I would not have been written up."

"But you would have missed you meeting with the gangster."

"Actually, there were two of them. They deliv-ered the stolen securities at JFK and have already pled guilty in the Eastern District."

---

Still worried, AUSA Rowan mentioned my letter to the United States Attorney. He asked to see it. Then he wrote her a letter of censure.

ADDRESS REPLY TO
"UNITED STATES ATTORNEY"
AND REFER TO
INITIALS AND NUMBER
WNS, Jr.

United States Department of Justice

UNITED STATES ATTORNEY
SOUTHERN DISTRICT OF NEW YORK
UNITED STATES COURTHOUSE
FOLEY SQUARE       ge
NEW YORK, N. Y. 10007

March 3, 1972

PERSONAL

Mrs. Harold W. Gossett II
United States Attorney's Office
New York, New York

Dear Mrs. Gossett:

In connection with a proposed change in your
personal status there was a failure on your part to
insure that necessary information pertinent to such
matters was furnished to this office in accordance
with existing regulations. Your explanation that you
were in love has been considered; however, it is apparent
that in this instance you failed to discharge your
responsibilities as an employee of this office, and
you were definitely at fault.

Very truly yours,

WHITNEY NORTH SEYMOUR, JR.
United States Attorney

P.S.    All kidding aside, congratulations and best
wishes for every happiness to you both.

WNS, JR.

We displayed these letters side by side in our living rooms for 48 years.

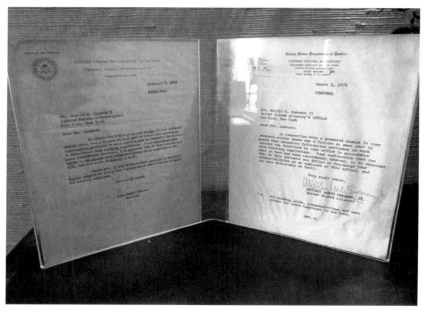

# CHAPTER EIGHT
# *Newlyweds*

"Sweetheart, I'm having difficulty using your name."

"You mean the roman numerals at the end?"

"No. I mean calling myself 'Mrs. Gossett.'"

"Want me to call myself, 'Mr. Rowan?'"

'No, silly. I have had charge accounts at Fifth Avenue stores for years, but when I asked to change my name on those, they insisted that I should have you fill out a credit application."

"How come?"

"Well, they say that you are now responsible for paying my debts, so they need to review your credit history and approve you as a customer."

"Did they give you the forms? I'll fill them out."

"Absolutely not. I'll just keep my 'Barbara Rowan' charge accounts."

"How about your Barbara Rowan checking account? We could have a joint account."

"No. I like having my own account. You can continue reconciling it every month, so you will always know how much money I have. Is that alright?"

"Sure. I just thought we could write one rent check every month and save one of us the trouble."

"I like writing my own checks. The landlord doesn't mind getting two checks. Is that okay with you?"

"Okay. No problem."

"Not okay. There is a problem."

"What's that?"

"I wrote to the New York State Bar and told them I would be practicing law as 'Barbara Ann Gossett' from now on. They wrote back and told me I would have to get your written permission to use your name."

"You're kidding."

"No, I'm not. Want to see their letter?"

"Of course not. What sort of document should I sign for them?"

"I have been practicing law for years. I don't need your permission to continue."

"So, you will be Attorney Barbara Ann Rowan at work and Mrs. Barbara Ann Gossett otherwise."

"That's correct. I have changed my last name on my driver's license. The State of New York doesn't think I need your permission to drive."

Some confusion about her surname followed Barbara all the way to her last day on earth, and beyond. She was registered in the hospital as Barbara Rowan, but the prepaid cremation was in the name Barbara Rowan Gossett, so the two organizations did not connect.

I was in the same Covid-19 Intensive Care Unit for an additional nine days after she passed away. I assumed the cremation society had taken her body to the crematorium.

A week after I got home, I received a call from a police officer who had been assigned to locate relatives to remove Miss Rowan's remains from the hospital. I resolved that problem as quickly as I could.

To be fair, we were in the middle of a pandemic, no vaccines were available, yet, Covid-19 was reaping lives in snowballing numbers, and our medical community was under enormous stress.

―――――――

"All I know how to make for dinner is reservations," Barbara had told me when we were dating.

After our wedding, I came home each evening to a superb meal.

"I thought you didn't know how to cook."

"I'm learning. I got some recipe books. What is your favorite food?"

"Greens."

"I don't do ethnic food."

"White people eat greens, too."

"Oh. I guess I'm not a racist. I'm a classist."

A few days later, I came home early and found Barbara in the kitchen on the telephone with her mom.

"Okay, it's boiling. Now what do I do?"

In a very few years she became an outstanding cook. I can count the only inedible thing she ever prepared on one finger. It was supposed to be sugar-free lime-flavored candy, but it turned out to be green glass.

To please me, she cooked a big pot of greens once a week for nearly five decades.

---

"Barbara, have you joined some strange religious cult, or are you going to be a clown at a child's birthday party?"

"What are you talking about?"

"The tip of your nose is all black. Is that some disease that White people know nothing about?"

"Oh!" She vigorously wiped the stuff off her nose. "That's the New York Times."

"You rubbed your nose on the New York Times? Are you punishing yourself for something?"

She laughed. "You know I'm nearsighted."

"So nearsighted that your nose touches the paper?"

"When I take my glasses off."

"Why would you take your glasses off?"

"To read faster."

"I can't even imagine how you see."

"I took a course in speed reading. I've got the stuff here somewhere. Want to learn?"

"I'd like to learn to read like normal people, but I'm dyslexic. I learned to read with two rulers, one above the line and one below."

"How does that help, Harry?"

"It keeps the letters from moving from one line to another."

"The letters move?"

"Yes, my love. They even move on the same line, but I can usually figure out the words."

"But you are so well-read."

"I may be well-informed, but I am not well-read."

"I can't imagine not being able to read faster than people talk."

"I even write faster than I can read."

"How is that possible?"

"I write with my hands, and I read with my eyes."

"I'll try to get my head around that, but in the meantime, don't let me leave the apartment with newsprint on my nose. Particularly not today."

"What's up today?"

"I'm appearing before a judge who chewed out one female lawyer for wearing a pants suit. He said she was 'trying to pass herself off as a man, and not doing a good job of it.'"

"What a jerk."

"Later, he objected to another woman wearing a dress, 'trying to take advantage of her femininity,' he said."

"There's no official dress code for women lawyers?"

"That would make it too easy."

"What are you going to wear?"

"I called his court clerk. He didn't think it would matter. He said, 'His honor always takes female lawyers to task for something.'"

I dropped in on Barbara's trial at the end of the day. She was wearing a nice business suit with a straight skirt.

The defense counsel was summing up. He apparently needed to divert the jury's attention away from the facts.

"I realize I'm old and ugly. And the government is represented here by an attractive young lady ..."

The judge said, "Aren't you going to object, Miss Rowan?"

"I have no objection to being called attractive, your honor."

The jury laughed.

The old ugly defense counsel pressed on. "When I was a young man, I wanted to be an Assistant United States Attorney. It was an important job then."

Barbara stood up. "I will object to that implied mischaracterization, your honor."

"Sustained. The judge turned to the defense counsel. "Summarize your case to the jury. And avoid *ad hominem* attacks on the prosecutrix."

*Prosecutrix?* I wondered if that were even a word.

It didn't take the jury long to find the accused "guilty as charged."

———

One winter weekend, we went to an outdoor firing range in the Poconos.

"You are surprisingly accurate with that pistol, young woman."

"You insisted I hold the gun with both hands, so I get to rest my arms on my boobs. How come you get to shoot with one hand, and I have to use two?"

"Because I'm trained for it."

"So, show me how."

"Okay."

———

"Andy, put an apostrophe in ODALE!" Barbara could hardly wait to tell me the funny things that had happened at her office. Andy was her Irish American boss.

"Who's O'Dale?"

"ODALE is not a who. It's The Office of Drug Abuse Law Enforcement."

"Did the Bureau of Narcotics and Dangerous Drugs change its name?"

"ODALE is President Nixon's invention. We'll have cops and postal inspectors, as well as agents from Customs and BNDD, all working together."

"I hope they can get along."

"Me too. I'm sort of heading up one of the units."

"What?"

"Each unit has an AUSA assigned. The commanders are expected to seek our legal advice before they take action."

"You gonna ride around with them?"

"Maybe. Half the units have federal agents in charge and half have ranking police officers. I guess it depends on how close they want us to be."

---

**Brrriiing!**

Our telephone was on my side of the bed, right next to our alarm clock showing it was just after 3:00 AM.

"Yeah?"

"Sorry to wake you, Mr. Rowan. This is Captain (let's call him 'O'Shaughnessy.' I don't remember his name, just his New York Irish accent). May I speak with your daughter?"

"I don't have a daughter."

"Oh. I think I rang the wrong number."

"You wanna talk to Barbara Rowan?"

"Yes. Is Miss Rowan there?"

"Sure. Wake up, honey, it's for you."

I laid the telephone on the pillow and heard the entire exchange.

"Hello. This is Miss Rowan."

"Sorry to wake you, Miss Rowan. This is Captain O'Shaughnessy, NYPD. First let me tell you how proud I am that an Irish girl such as yourself has such an important job."

"I'm sure you didn't wake me up to tell me that. What can I do for you?"

"Well, we took down some spades on 125th Street and they had a big German Shepard who bit one of the federal agents. We've secured the vicious cur with duct tape. Can we charge him with Assaulting a Federal Officer?"

"No. We can't charge a dog."

"Okay. We'll just shoot him then."

"Good Lord, No! Don't shoot the dog! If the arrestees don't have a relative handy who can take custody, put the dog in an animal shelter."

"This is an attack dog, Miss."

"Let the animal welfare folks decide what to do with the dog. What about the agent who was injured?"

"I've had him transported to the hospital, Miss. He's not seriously wounded. Thanks for asking."

"Put the prisoners in the West Street Jail and stop by my office in the morning. We'll decide what to charge them with."

"Good night to you, Miss, or rather, good morning."

As I hung up the phone, Barbara said, "I can't wait to see the captain's face when he meets *me* in the morning."

---

"Did you meet Captain O'Shaughnessy this morning?"

"I did."

"So?"

"So, he bounded into my office and said, 'please find this Rowan girl.'

'I am the Rowan girl.'

'Ah Jesus.'

"After an awkward pause, he said, 'I've gotten off on the wrong foot with you, Miss Rowan. I'm sure we can work together. What can I do to make it right? Would you like a car and driver?'

'A White driver?'

'That can be arranged.'

"He's very quick and funny. We're gonna get along fine."

"Are you really gonna hit the street with your crew?"

"I don't think so. But could I have that Colt Detective Special. It works much smoother than any of your Smith & Wessons."

"You're gonna carry a gun now?"

"Yes."

"Did your boss approve this?"

"No. But I'm a federal law enforcement officer."

"Who's not authorized to carry."

"I won't shoot anyone who doesn't need shooting."

"I don't want you to go to jail."

"You know what they say: 'It's better to be judged by twelve than carried by six.'"

———————

Early in the Spring, I took Barbara to Missouri to meet my parents.

In the small hours of the morning, our headlights lit up the universal gloom of the community where I grew up.

As I pulled into the back yard, Barbara asked, "Shouldn't we go to a hotel and come back in the morning?"

"I can honk, if you want to make sure they are awake."

"No. Don't wake the entire neighborhood." She was surprised that the back door was unlocked (as it had been throughout my lifetime).

I walked her through the house in the darkness, opened my parent's bedroom door and said, "Sorry to show up at this hour, mom and dad. Our flight was delayed."

They muttered something indicating they knew I was there.

"I want you to meet my wife, Barbara."

My mom said, "Hi, Barbara."

"We'll see her in the morning," said my dad.

I led Barbara to my old bedroom. Once we were in bed, she said, "I can't wait to hear what they'll say when they see me in daylight." She was genuinely concerned.

"I can't wait, either. They're gonna love you."

And they did. From the moment they met her until they died.

In fact, I don't know anyone who ever met Barbara who didn't like her. I know folks who don't care for me, but no one who didn't adore my marvelous wife.

---

"Aww. How sweet." Barbara extended her arms and walked toward a bear cub who had rolled out of the bushes and plopped down on the Appalachian Trail right in front of us.

I grabbed my wife's left shoulder with my left hand. "Stop! That baby's got a momma around here somewhere." With my right hand, I drew my ankle gun, a five shot .38 Smith & Wesson Chief Special. I thought, "*This is just enough fire-power to make a bear go berserk.*" I was swiveling my head and hoping that the mother was not behind me.

Wump! A second little bear tumbled onto the path. It stood up and turned toward us. After an electrifying pause, the adult appeared, followed by a third cub.

Momma bear immediately went into attack mode, roaring at us and slapping the ground.

I rested my gun hand on Barbara's right shoulder and took careful aim at the animal's snarling mouth, the only place a .38 round might make a difference. As I slowly pressed the trigger, the hammer crept back. I held fast, thinking the muzzle blast might take out Barbara's best eye and the loud report would leave her deaf in her right ear.

My target did not advance. One at a time, she kicked her offspring off the trail, and then shut up and followed them down the hill.

I eased off the trigger and lowered my pistol.

Barbara and I hugged for several minutes.

That night, a mosquito got into our borrowed tent and Barbara tore the tent down trying to kill it.

"I can't believe you, baby. This afternoon you faced down an angry bear, and tonight you go crazy over a little mosquito."

"I hate bugs, particularly flying insects."

"I'm not crazy about mosquitoes either."

"While you put Dave's tent back up, I'll get something out of the car which will keep the little blood suckers out."

She brought back a Mosquito Citronella Coil and lit it. We slept in the smell which insects avoid. Unfortunately, one of us kicked it off its little stand and set the tent on fire. We spent the rest of the night outside bundled together in the one big sleeping bag that we were able to make by zipping two together.

Of course, we bought my squad-mate, Dave, a new tent. And we bought ourselves one, too.

Ever after, in a humorous mode, my wife liked to tell people that when we encountered an angry bear, I held her in front of me so she would be eaten first.

That gave me the opportunity to recount the big city woman's first reaction to meeting a wild bear cub. She tried to pick it up.

---

"Want to play softball, Harry?"

"Where?"

"My office has organized a softball outing and spouses are invited."

"You gonna play?"

"Of course."

"Count me in."

By then I knew my nearsighted wife was right-handed and had only 20/400 vision in her left eye. I hoped that not being able to hit a softball, in front of all the men she worked with, would not be too humiliating for her.

Players were divided into two teams. Barbara and I were on the same side.

When it was our turn to bat, I was up first. I struck out. So did the next two batters. The opposing pitcher was terrific.

The next inning was also three up and three down. No one even got a foul tip of that demon.

Then Barbara was our lead-off batter.

I whispered in her ear, "Don't crowd the plate, darling. You may not see the ball in time to duck."

"I'll be careful."

The first pitch came in fast, high, and inside, right at her face. She took two steps back—and smacked it right out of the park!

After her stroll around the bases, I asked her, "How did you learn to hit like that?"

"I had to. It's too embarrassing to run if you have a chest like mine."

# CHAPTER NINE
## *Fall in Canada*

"Listen to this, Barbara." I dialed the phone and we put our heads together.

"*Bonjour, Gendarmerie royale du Canada.* Good Morning, Royal Canadian Mounted Police."

I asked for an inspector that I was friends with. While they were tracking him down, Barbara asked, "Did you want me to listen in on your call?"

"I just wanted you to hear how they answer the phone, in two languages."

"He's in Québec, right?"

I nodded.

"They do everything in French and English in Québec."

"You've been there before?"

"When I was little."

I told my Mounty friend that we were coming to Canada for a short vacation. He was delighted and promised to show us some of the highlights of Montréal.

I bought two cots and packed them in the trunk of our rental car, before I double-parked in front of our apartment building. There I stuffed in our pop tent, sleeping bags, Coleman stove, etc. while Barbara filled a military-surplus seabag with clothing.

We went to Portland, Maine, where we drove onto a ferry to Nova Scotia.

Deck passage turned out to be a big mistake. As the boat crossed the Bay of Fundy, the icy wind cut right through our winter clothes.

"Matty! What are you doing here?"

The DEA agent was equally surprised to see Barbara.

"I was about to ask you the same thing."

"We're freezing," I said. "How do you stay so warm?"

"I have a cabin. Want to come in and get warm?"

Barbara asked, "Can we do that? We are only deck passengers."

"It's *my* cabin. I should be able to entertain my friends there."

I said, "What's the worst that could happen? If they throw us in the brig, it will be warmer than out here."

Our good friend Matty stayed up all night with us, in the bar and then in his cozy quarters. It turned out he had been a professional baseball player in Canada and returned frequently to go fishing.

Shortly after dawn, the ship docked in Nova Scotia.

As we were waiting for the gang plank to be lowered, Barbara asked, "Where do you guys carry your pistols? I can't see them."

I said, "We don't carry guns in Canada."

"I do," she said, patting her coat pocket.

Matty asked, "Who do you think you are? Che Guevara?"

I said, "Take a walk with me around to the other side of the ship so the officials can't see us and drop that revolver in the bay."

"I will not. This is *my* gun."

"It was mine till I gave it to you. I'll give you another one when we get home."

"No. This one is lighter and has a much smoother action than any of your other revolvers."

Matty said, "I'll call the U.S. Embassy and tell them where you're incarcerated, before I take off on my fishing trip."

Fortunately, metal detectors were not used in those days. We glided through the customs and immigration check points with no trouble.

Barbara and I drove around Cape Breton Island. The forest there had been burned to the ground. Just charred trunks of trees still stood.

Canada looked better as we drove west. We camped a third of the way across Canada during our two-week vacation.

---

"How come you didn't tell me you speak French?"

"Because I don't."

"Barbara, I just watched you carry on a conversation with those other campers for at least five minutes."

"We were just talking about the nice bathrooms and hot showers they have here in their campgrounds."

"In French."

"Well, Canadian French. You know the Parisians always tease them about how they handle the language."

"No, I didn't know that."

"It's like some uppity Brits don't think Americans speak English."

"So, you speak some form of French. Right?"

"Not much. I could never discuss philosophy or anything complicated."

"I can't even ask 'which way to the nice clean restroom.'"

"I can teach you that."

———————

We met with a few of my Mountie friends in Québec City and Montréal. Their kids were awed to meet a real FBI agent while my wife was just as star struck by meeting real Mounties.

One evening we had dinner with a group of Mounties and their wives. As we left the restaurant, we passed one of them speaking on the phone.

Outside, I said, "I'll bet you had difficulty understanding his French. Didn't even sound like French to me."

"Because it wasn't. He was speaking Russian."

Later, I learned his parents were Russian immigrants to Canada.

----

Throughout this trip, Miss Rowan carried her Colt Detective Special concealed on her person, in various ways. Having no holster, she never found a comfortable place to put it.

Another thing she didn't enjoy on that trip was sleeping on the ground when we camped. She didn't mention that until we got home, and I unloaded the cots I had purchased before we left.

"You had cots in the trunk! And you made me sleep on the cold hard ground!"

"You didn't know we had these army cots? I thought you liked snuggling on the ground."

"Next time, we'll sleep on our cots. Okay?"

"Okay."

As it happened, we camped out over a hundred times, and we never used those cots.

# CHAPTER TEN
## *Life and Work Collide*

***Smack! Smack!*** "Please! Please!" ***Smack! Smack!*** "Leroy! You're hurting me!"

My head snapped around.

Barbara grabbed my arm. "Don't get involved."

We had just left a movie theater that Friday night and were walking home up Third Avenue when we heard a woman screaming, just a few feet to our left on 87th Street. A man was holding her up against a *No Parking* signpost with his left hand on her throat while he slapped her face with his right.

I shook off my wife and grabbed his slapping hand.

"Let her go, Leroy."

"Ain't none of your business."

I released his wrist and showed him my credentials.

He was not intimidated. "Ain't no federal crime."

***Smack! Smack!***

I grabbed him again, and said, "It's not a federal crime, but it is a breach of the peace."

"Still ain't none of your business."

The victim wriggled free and ran west on 87th Street. I held Leroy.

"Yes, it is. I live in this neighborhood. You wanna slap your woman, you do that in your neighborhood."

"You gonna let go of me?"

"Not till she gets to Lexington Avenue." I figured that would give the gal a 900-foot head start.

Once she turned that corner, I let the man go.

He didn't seem to be in a hurry as he marched in her direction.

Barbara and I followed.

When we turned onto Lexington Avenue, we discovered Leroy and his victim kissing passionately in a parked car.

"See that!" Barbara barked at me. "If he had stabbed you back there, they would still be right here kissing."

"I couldn't just let him slap her teeth out."

"I don't want to lose you, Harry. Certainly not due to two stupid jerks like them."

"In the future, don't grab my gun hand, okay?"

We calmed down before bedtime. We never, ever, went to bed angry with one another.

---

"Hey, sweetie. Do you know a BNDD agent named Frank Tummillo?"

"No."

"How about one named Thomas Devine?"

"I know Tom. He's a Group Supervisor. Why are you asking me about them?"

"They got shot last night. I'm working the case as Assault on a Federal Officer violations."

"Oh, no. Were they killed?"

"Tummillo was. Devine took a round in his neck that shattered his spine. I think he is still alive."

"What hospital is he in?"

"I don't know. If he survives, I may have to interview him. Right now, I'm working with two inspectors from DEA trying to put the pieces together."

"What happened?"

"Looks like an undercover buy turned out to be an attempted rip-off by the bad guys and about 40 rounds were exchanged in a hotel room."

"Any other agents wounded?"

"I don't think so. Both bad guys were killed at the scene. We'll be looking to identify any co-conspirators."

---

"It's been a long day," I said from the back seat.

"Yeah, said one of the inspectors, but the two of us aren't getting much sleep till we wrap this up."

***Smack! Smack!*** "OW! OW! Leroy! Please!" ***Smack! Smack!***

I looked to my right and there was Leroy slapping the same woman he had been smacking the week before. He had her pinned against a parked car.

Since we were stuck at a long traffic light, I asked the inspectors if they would turn on the loudspeaker and hand me the microphone.

"LEROY." My voice boomed.

Leroy looked straight up, as though he had been addressed by God himself.

"LEROY. OVER HERE." I lowered my window so he could see me. "WHAT DID I TELL YOU ABOUT HITTING HER, LEROY?"

"You said to hit her in my neighborhood." He pointed with his slapping hand. "I live right here!"

The light changed. I handed the microphone back to a puzzled DEA inspector and said, "We can't protect a willing victim."

Still focused on their colleagues who had been shot, the driver grunted, and we rolled away.

―――――――――

"Hey, Harry, did you have any dinner?"

"No, I've been putting a major push on the assault case."

"Let me warm up something for you."

"Yeah, I'll take a shower while you do that. You'll never guess who I ran into tonight."

"Someone I know?"

"Sort of. Do you remember Leroy, that guy who was slapping his gal last Friday night?"

"She obviously likes to be smacked."

"How perceptive you are, my darling. Tonight, he had her up against a parked car, slapping the snot out of her. We got stopped in traffic right there for the main event."

"I hope you didn't get involved, again."

"Not much. I used the loudspeaker. When I said, 'LEROY,' he looked straight up."

"Did he let her go?"

"Remember when I told him to slap her in his neighborhood?"

"Don't tell me you were in his neighborhood."

"Right in front of his residence."

"I hope you gave him permission to continue."

"Tacitly. When the light changed, we just drove away."

"You did the right thing, sweetheart."

"Yeah. I hope they only do their act on Friday nights, and that she has dental insurance."

"She obviously likes to be hit."

"He could have the common decency to smack her bottom, not her face."

"Hmm. I guess her bruised cheeks wouldn't be exposed to the whole world that way. Did you get any word on Tom's condition?"

"I'm pretty sure he's still alive. Someone would have let us know if he died."

"I tried to visit him at the hospital, but he is not able to have visitors, yet."

"What's the prognosis?"

"They wouldn't tell us anything."

"Us?"

"There was a herd of BNDD personnel there," she said.

"Family?"

"I guess. I didn't ask everyone who they were."

---

"Are you awake, sir?"

Every appendage of the corpse on the bed was strapped down securely, particularly his head. His eyes popped open and rolled my way.

I identified myself. "I'm Special Agent Gossett from the FBI."

"Hi, Harry. Miss Rowan said you might need to interview me."

"Ahma...hama..." I was taken aback.

"You're her husband, right?" The eyes of the dying man were twinkling, and he was smiling at me!

"Barbara got in here?"

"I don't know how."

His impish expression made me grin.

"I guess she charmed her way in," he said.

"She never ceases to amaze me."

"You are one lucky man, Harry, to be married to such a wonderful woman."

I would hear those sentiments for the rest of her life from myriad people, but it was surrealistic to be discussing my wife's wonderfulness with a total stranger on his deathbed.

"Do you remember the shooting?" I asked.

"Absolutely. Since they had left to go get the drugs, I walked into the room to check on my agent. They had slipped back in and had Frank Tummillo with a gun to his head. The other one shot me. I was lying on the floor looking up at the creep and I couldn't move. My body was frozen. I realized I was at his mercy, and he didn't have any."

Tom recalled every word spoken and every shot fired. Although totally incapacitated, he could hear, and his brain was in high gear.

Although his bullet wound left Special Agent Supervisor Thomas Devine a quadriplegic, he survived, and he continued as a Group Supervisor, in a non-enforcement role, in an intelligence group in the Bureau of Narcotics and Dangerous Drugs. Retaining him was a brilliant move by someone in charge.

When BNDD was merged into the newly formed Drug Enforcement Administration, DEA kept him on. I give them high marks for that.

Like so many people who populated Barbara's life, she stayed in touch with Tom Devine.

He passed away ten years after the gun battle in the hotel room that crippled his body, but not his marvelous mind.

# CHAPTER ELEVEN
## *My Christmas Lessons*

"We've got an invite to another Christmas party, Barbara."

"I hate parties."

"I know. But since I've been doing liaison work with the First Deputy Commissioner's Office, we've been asked to attend the Chiefs' Christmas Party."

"Big event, huh?"

"Yeah. The NYPD has lots of chiefs: Chief of Patrol, chief of this, chief of that, perhaps two dozen chiefs. Guests from other agencies, like you and me, will be there, too."

"I suppose we have to go."

"I think we should.

---

Barbara and I were seated at a table with three chiefs and their wives.

The guest speaker was a judge with a heavy Italian accent. His speech was very pro law enforcement, and he received a standing ovation.

As he walked back to his table, he saw Barbara at the far side of the ballroom. He marched right over to her, and they chatted merrily.

When he walked away, the woman sitting next to Barbara turned to her and said, "I knew it. You're Italian."

"Why would you think that?" My wife asked.

"You were speaking to the judge in Italian."

"No. He was telling me a joke in Portuguese."

"That it! You're Portuguese."

"No."

The band began to play. I pulled Barbara away from her interrogator. "Let's dance, honey."

On the dance floor, Barbara explained that the judge was born in New York, but his family moved back to Italy when he was a baby. While growing up there, he learned several languages, "but English the worst."

He came back to New York to attend college and law school, became an Assistant District Attorney and later a judge.

When Barbara was a court interpreter, she occasionally worked in his courtroom. He often addressed the defendants in their own languages. Sometimes the defense attorneys didn't know what he was saying to their clients, so Barbara translated for the lawyers as well as for the record.

We returned to our table and, as soon as we sat down, the woman next to Barbara said, "Persian. You're Persian, right?"

"No."

This time, the nosy neighbor's husband took her away to dance.

I whispered to Barbara, "While you are safely rid of her for the moment, I'll find a phone and do a message check."

The switchboard operator at the FBI office told me a confidential informant was awaiting my call on an urgent matter. I called him. It was urgent.

I pulled Barbara away from the table and made a quick apology. The police chiefs and their wives were not shocked or offended that duty called.

Trudging through a light snowfall, I explained to Barbara that the confidential source kept tabs on a domestic terrorist group, and he needed to meet me in person. I had chosen a street corner two blocks away from the Christmas party.

"Which domestic terrorist group?" she asked.

"Can't say, but I can tell you they have attacked foreign diplomatic missions and even fired rounds into a women's college. Their founder was convicted of conspiracy to manufacture explosives and they are now planning a bombing."

"Ah, Meir Kahane and the Jewish Defense League."

"Damn you're smart."

"It was the women's college that gave it away, honey. Hunter College, right?"

"Yeah. I guess most terrorists don't shoot at college women."

"Most rabbis are not like Meir Kahane."

The source showed up in a two-seat sports car.

"Hi, Harry. I didn't know you were going to bring a friend."

"This is my wife, Rabbi. She is also an Assistant United States Attorney."

"I want to show you where the [he used a Yiddish obscenity to identify the members of the Jewish Defense League] will be meeting tomorrow night. Can she wait here. It will only take a minute."

"I could take a vacation on one of your minutes, chum."

Barbara said, "It's okay, Harry. I've got a warm coat."

I hopped in and he drove me a few blocks to point out where the terrorists would hold their secret meeting. He knew we had no arrest warrants, yet, but surveillance was a certainty now that we knew when and where they would gather.

We returned to Barbara's corner and pulled up right behind a police car. We could hear the officer saying, to my very well-dressed wife, "Move it along, honey."

"Why?" asked Barbara. "I'm standing on a public sidewalk."

"You can't work on my beat. You want to go to jail?"

Barbara was facing away from me. She didn't see me approaching.

She told the officer, "I am waiting for my husband, so I must stay right here."

"You can meet your pimp somewhere else."

At that point I joined the conversation. "What's the problem, officer?"

"Move it along, pal. Police business."

"If it involves my wife, it's my business." I displayed my FBI credentials.

He caught his breath. "Sorry pal."

As we watched the police car roll away, I said, "Come on, sweetheart, we are going back to the party."

"Why?"

"Because one of those chiefs is his."

"No, no, no. Please don't make an issue of this."

"Of course, I'm going to make an issue of this. That cop can't get away with talking to you like that."

"Just forget it. Please."

"Why do you want me to forget it?"

"Because he will lie about it, the police will believe him, and it will spoil your relationship with the NYPD."

While I stood there with snowflakes bouncing off my face thinking about her argument, she added, "I'm Black. This is not the first time something like this has happened to me. And to pretty much everyone else who's Black."

I finally agreed to pretend it never happened.

We had a fireplace in our little apartment with a fake bearskin rug in front of it, on which we sometimes snuggled in front of the fire.

"Barbara, we've been married for almost a year now."

"I know. I'm just as surprised as you are."

"I'm not surprised."

"You plan to keep me, eh?"

"Please don't tell me that color is in the eye of the beholder. Your skin is getting whiter every day."

She laughed. "Is that why you stare at me when I'm naked?"

"No. But while I'm ogling your bare body, I keep noticing that you've faded."

"You think you are rubbing off on me?"

"You think I'm crazy."

"No. I think that, like most White people, you don't realize Black people get suntanned, too."

"So next summer you will be my chocolate baby again?"

"Maybe not as dark as when we met. I had just returned from sailing in the Caribbean."

"So, you change colors with the seasons?"

"Yes. But I'm always Black on the inside, even when Black people can't tell…until I speak to them with a Black accent."

"I've noticed you sound different when you speak to Black people."

"I grew up in a Black neighborhood, but I work in a White world."

Thus, I observed how both White people and Black people treated Barbara differently depending on her skin color. At the end of winter, White people were warm and friendly while Black people were wary. At the end of each summer, the reverse was true.

# CHAPTER TWELVE
## *Duty Supervisors*

"Barbara, perhaps you can help me."

"To do what?"

"Catch a fugitive."

"How can I help?"

"Well, I have this UFAP warrant for a woman whose mom lives near yours."

"What did she do?"

"Unlawful Flight to Avoid Prosecution."

"I know what UFAP means. What was her underlying crime? Are you walking me into a gun battle?"

"I would never endanger you, baby. My subject was one of several people who committed frauds in Atlanta. After being arrested and charged, she fled to New York."

"Staying at her mom's place?"

"Her mom told me she doesn't live there. I explained that all the co-defendants got probation, so if her daughter turns herself in, she probably won't go to jail. But if she doesn't, she might also be prosecuted for unlawful flight and then she very well could do time."

"Did you threaten to arrest her mother for harboring a fugitive?"

"Absolutely not. I learned my lesson the hard way when I was a rookie agent. After I told a mother she could be prosecuted for harboring, she hit me over the head with a frying pan. I asked my very experienced partner why he didn't arrest her for assaulting a federal officer. He laughed and said, 'No jury is gonna convict a mother for harboring her kid.'"

"I'm guessing the woman was White and the fugitive was her son, not her daughter."

"Exactly."

"It could go very differently for a Black family. You want me to talk to the mother, right?"

"I do. I don't think she believed me, but an Assistant United States Attorney who grew up in her neighborhood might be more credible than a White FBI agent."

"When do we do this?"

After we do your mom's grocery shopping next Saturday."

———————

"Good afternoon, ma'am. I'm Harry Gossett. I'm an FBI agent. I explained to your mom last week that I have a federal arrest warrant with your name on it."

"Oh, no!"

The fugitive's mother appeared behind her. "I told you not to answer the door!"

I addressed the distraught mother. "I suggested that your daughter turn herself in, but she didn't."

"She will! I swear. You don't have to arrest her."

"I'm an Assistant United States Attorney," Barbara told the women. "Special Agent Gossett has no discretion in this matter. An arrest warrant is a forthwith court order. He can't walk away from a fugitive."

As I handcuffed the angry outlaw, I started explaining her rights and leading her out the door, leaving her weeping mother behind.

We took the subway to the FBI office, staffed at night and on the weekends by a Duty Supervisor and support personnel.

While I was filling out the paperwork concerning my arrestee, the Duty Supervisor asked, "Who's that woman with the prisoner?"

"That's my wife."

Barbara said, "I'm an Assistant United States Attorney."

The Duty Supervisor told her, "That doesn't matter." And to me he said, "You can't take you wife on an arrest."

Barbara said, "He didn't take me on an arrest. He took me grocery shopping and we ran into a fugitive."

I asked the Duty Supervisor, "What did you expect me to do?"

"Harrumph!"

---

On our walk home, I said, "You should have let me do the talking."

"I would have, but you didn't say anything."

"I didn't have a chance. You spoke up before I could get my mouth open."

"That's because I'm a New Yorker and you're a hillbilly."

"You're right. But next time, could you take a breath and give me a chance?"

"No, I'm afraid not. That's not in my nature. Here people make comments in passing. You don't have time to compose a response. That's why all the great one-liners come from New York."

Throughout our lives together, Barbara's verbal counterpunches were always a full second or two ahead of mine, and frequently made antagonists laugh.

---

"Are you still scheduled to be the Duty AUSA tonight?"

"Yeah. Starting in two hours. If you need an urgent legal opinion after five, give me another call then, Special Agent Gossett."

"I was thinking about giving you a ride, AUSA Rowan."

"I can get a ride from DEA anytime."

"You're not married to a DEA agent."

"So how come you've got a car?"

"We only have 70 cars for 1,100 agents, so I had to wait my turn just like everybody else."

"And now you don't know what to do with it?"

"On the contrary, my darling. I have a conman fugitive I've been looking for, so I drove around Brooklyn all day visiting his Jewish family. But none of them have seen him today."

"I'm impressed with you, goy boy. You knew tonight starts Passover, right?"

"I did."

"So, you want to know if you can arrest him at a Seder?"

"No. I hadn't planned on that. What I would like to do is stop by his apartment in Manhattan, again. He wasn't there this morning, but since he's not with his relatives, he might be home."

"Taking your wife on another arrest, are you?"

"I'm still trying to explain away the last time I did that. I've got Bobby with me. You can stay in the car."

"In case you need a legal opinion?"

"Right. If we catch the swindler, there's a subway stop a block from the building. You can take the train."

---

"Holy Cannoli! A parking space!"

"It's a fire plug," Barbara said from the back seat.

"That's okay. You'll be in the car. Got your creds with you?"

"I'm not sure a meter maid is going to be impressed that I'm a government lawyer."

"We won't be long. He's either there or he's not. Come on Bobby, that woman with the shopping bags is headed toward the door."

After the resident opened the door, my partner and I followed her in chatting about the stock market. I jingled my keys in one hand as though I were getting my apartment door key ready. The resident couldn't possibly know all her neighbors in the high-rise apartment building.

Upstairs I rang the doorbell and a young man's voice asked who was there.

"Harry Gossett. I talked to you this morning. Showed you the warrant for your roommate. We need to look around, again."

"Uh…I don't think so."

"Think again."

"But you already looked."

"He may have gone out this morning and returned this evening. Come on, kid. Open the door."

"I told you I don't know where he is."

"Believe it or not, sometimes people lie to me to protect their friends."

"You can't keep coming back here."

"Actually, I can."

"Is that legal? Should I call my lawyer?"

"You have a lawyer?"

"I know a lawyer I can call."

"Okay, we'll wait a minute while you call your lawyer."

Bobby whispered to me, "Your fugitive is in there."

I nodded.

A few minutes later, the lad informed us, "My lawyer says you had a look, and you don't get another one."

"He obviously doesn't appreciate your position here. Please call him back and tell him that there are law enforcement officers at your door who will break it down and possibly arrest you for obstruction. While you do that, I'll contact the U.S. Attorney's office and find out if I have to arrest you or not."

"Okay."

I left my partner to guard the door, took the elevator down, propped the front door open, and described the situation to AUSA Rowan.

"Are you sure this is the same young man who saw your credentials and the warrant this morning?"

"Absolutely."

"Well, if you have to kick the door down, you can arrest him whether or not the fugitive is in there."

I failed to mention to her that it was not a door that could be kicked down. We would need implements which we didn't have at the scene.

Earlier I had spotted a pay phone around the corner. It was out of Barbara's sight, so she didn't see me call my office. I asked the Duty Supervisor to send someone with a sledgehammer.

"I don't have anyone here I can spare," he said. "I'll call Emergency Services for you."

Back upstairs at the apartment door, I told the young fellow, "We are waiting for a sledgehammer."

He sounded nervous but didn't open the door.

Suddenly, 8 or 10 uniformed police officers with a couple of shotguns were all around us.

I explained the situation to their leader. He shouted to the young man inside, "You are obstructing governmental administration. Open this door right now or we are going to break it down."

He looked at his watch for a minute and then gave a nod to a 300-pound officer with a 50-pound sledgehammer, who gave the lock one loud WHACK! The bent metal door swung open. We flooded the apartment. The young man I had met that morning was the only occupant.

He said, "The lock came off the door, flew right by my face. Lucky the balcony door was open. It sailed right out there."

"Okay, kid. You are under arrest for obstruction. Put your hands on the wall while I pat you down."

"My lawyer said not to talk to you."

"I see no reason to interview you at all. But I would like you to call your lawyer again."

"Why? He doesn't know where ..."

"Because your door can't be locked in its current condition. He needs to call a locksmith and get it fixed. And he'll need to be in court in the morning. Tell him it's the Federal District Court, Southern District."

The Emergency Services Officers vanished as quickly as they had appeared.

---

Outside the FBI office, Bobby stayed with the double-parked car because there were no legal parking spaces available.

I said, "Miss Rowan, I'm going to ask you to come upstairs with me while we process the prisoner."

"I'll let you do the talking, Special Agent Gossett."

"Good idea."

The Duty Supervisor was not the one Barbara had met last time. He reviewed my paperwork and said, "You didn't fill in the part about the warrant."

"This was a probable cause arrest, a crime committed in my presence."

"Who authorized it?"

"AUSA Rowan."

One of his support persons whispered in his ear. That young man had witnessed Barbara's last confrontation with a different Duty Supervisor."

"Isn't AUSA Rowan your wife?"

"Yes, she is the Duuu…"

"You can't get an opinion from your wife! You have to call a real AUSA."

"I *am* a real AUSA!" Barbara stepped right up to his desk. "I am the Duty AUSA tonight, just like you are the Duty Supervisor. I can give you the U.S. Attorney's home number if you would like to call and confirm that he put me in charge."

"Um…hmmm…No, that…that won't be necessary."

Fortunately, our arrestee was being photographed upstairs during this clash.

Barbara took the subway home while Bobby and I lodged the lad in the West Street Jail.

When I walked into our apartment, Barbara grabbed me in a bear hug.

"Oh, Harry, I was so scared."

That was so out-of-character for her.

"What? … When? … Why?"

"After you said you were gonna kick the door down, you left me in the car for a very long time. Then a whole herd of policemen ran into the building. With shotguns! Then something crashed on top of the car in front of yours. It wasn't big enough to be you, but something violent was going on up there."

"Ah. That was the locking mechanism from the apartment door. The biggest cop I've ever seen hit it with the biggest sledgehammer I've ever seen. It came off the inside of the door, sailed across the living room, and over the balcony. Did you get the tag number of that car?"

"No. Why?"

"We can pay for damages, so long as the people don't sue us."

"Oh?"

"If they sue, they get whatever they get or don't get in court."

"How about if I have a heart attack? Is the Bureau gonna pay for that?"

"Sweetheart, I'm so proud of you. I didn't know you were frightened at all. I'm sure no one else did either."

While we waited for the magistrate in his courtroom the next morning, Barbara whispered, "The only precedents I could find were under the Fugitive Slave act. How embarrassing is that?"

An infamous Mafia defense lawyer showed up to represent the young man I had arrested.

After reading what Barbara had written, the judge didn't raise any issues of law. He asked the defense counsel, "Are you the lawyer who told this defendant not to open the door when you knew there were armed law enforcement officers threating to break it down?"

"That's right. This agent right here had been…"

"Stop!" The magistrate raised his hand. He looked to our side of the courtroom. "I am dismissing this case, because you have arrested the wrong man." He turned back to the belligerent lawyer, who said, "I took those calls in Brooklyn. I wasn't in the Southern District."

"Shut up!"

"The FBI broke the door and left it open all night, and…"

"You should have secured your client's quarters. That was the least you could do after causing him to be arrested."

The mob mouthpiece finally decided to take his win and leave quietly. Otherwise, he might have clanked from the courtroom.

Later, I learned that the fugitive I was hunting had been in the apartment during both my visits. He had installed a fake wall with a peephole so a person concealed there could see the sucker's cards and signal the dealer during high stakes poker games held in the living room. That's where he hid when the FBI came calling.

---

"Signal 2133 responding."

"Does stuff like this happen every night?"

"Only when you are the Duty AUSA."

This time we were going up 10th Avenue on Manhattan's westside when the office advised that a robbery had been interrupted in Brooklyn, the robbers had shot police officers, and were holding hostages in a sporting goods store with unlimited guns and ammunition.

Jurisdiction is irrelevant when law enforcement officers need help.

"Roll down you window and put the fireball on the roof."

I turned on the siren while she put the red flasher on top of the car.

"Pull the cigarette lighter and plug the cord in there."

"Nobody is getting out of the way." Barbara was surprised.

"Welcome to New York. These people hear sirens 24/7."

"I'm one of these people and I would get out of the way."

"You're a good citizen."

I turned right on 42nd Street and we came alongside a NYPD cruiser.

"Who yous guys?" an officer shouted.

"FBI. Going to Brooklyn."

"Good luck with that," he shouted back.

After we were out of his earshot, Barbara giggled, and mocked his accent, "Who yous guys," *tee hee*.

"He just wanted to know if we were responding to an emergency in his sector that the NYPD didn't know about."

"I see."

"I'm gonna drop you at Central Station. This hostage situation could go on for days. They're not gonna run out of bullets and we are not going to refuse to send in food for the hostages."

"And you don't want to explain me to the Duty Supervisor."

"And you won't have to explain why the Southern District Duty AUSA wound up in the Eastern District."

"Yeah. That too."

# CHAPTER THIRTEEN
# *Naughty Movies*

"I want to go to a porno movie."

Those were the last words I expected to ever hear from my well-behaved apostle of etiquette. "Any particular skin flick?

"Absolutely. It's called '*Deep Throat.*'"

I chuckled. "You know the story line? It's about a woman who was born with her clitoris in her throat, so she gets off giving head jobs."

"Hmm. I won't ask you how you know that."

"It was obviously written by a guy. Why do you want to see it?"

"Well, the Supreme Court has never defined obscenity, so judges are left to decide if something is obscene, or not, on a case-by-case basis."

(Later that year, 1973, the U.S. Supreme Court set up a test for obscenity in **Miller v. California**.)

"Don't tell me a judge has assigned you the task of determining if *Deep Throat* is obscene."

"No. Judge Tyler assigned himself that task. I want to see it before he makes his ruling."

"Oooo. We're in a racy race."

"Aren't you interested?"

"More like confused."

"About what?"

"When I worked in the Kansas City office, one of my jobs was to burn the FBI trash. There was a big furnace in the basement of the courthouse. The Postal Inspectors would be down there burning porno magazines, and risqué post cards, and stuff like that."

"They let you have a look?"

"Of course. But I also wanted to know what their standards were. The Sears catalogue has pictures of women and children in their underwear. That wasn't considered obscene."

"Do you still have that list?"

"They didn't give me a list, but I remember the most common violations. Pubic hair, action pictures…"

"*Action* pictures? What kind of action?"

"Oh, something like a picture of someone who seems to have their face on someone else's genitals."

"And those naughty pictures left you confused?"

"Not those. The pictures in the form book down at your office."

"What form book?"

"You have a book of examples for different kinds of documents. The one I'm talking about is the Search Warrant Application. The exemplar was a case from the Postal Inspectors here in New York. The attached evidence was a bunch of pictures of women in their underwear. Well, they were wearing jewelry and high heels, too."

"You're telling me that the Southern District of New York is more prudish than the federal court in Kansas City?"

"Looks that way to me."

---

"This is where we came in, Barbara."

"Yeah. We know how it ends. Let's get out of here."

As we pushed past knees to get to the aisle, a little old woman said, "What's the matter, honey? Too much for you?"

Barbara said, "No. We've seen it four times and we have to get home before the babysitter leaves."

Everyone within earshot laughed aloud.

A day or so later, one of the New York newspapers had the huge headline **JUDGE CUTS THROAT**.

Judge Tyler ranted about the gross obscenity and fined the producers $100,000.

---

"Hi, Harry. This is Elliot. You and Barbara have got to go see a movie called '*China Blue*.'"

"Why?"

"Just go. You'll know why in the first 30 seconds."

"What's it about?"

"Mostly naked sex."

"I'm gonna need more than the fact that you liked it to get Barbara to go see an adult film."

"No, you don't. Just tell her I guaranteed she will be interested."

Elliot and Barbara were law school classmates and had shared office space in Greenwich Village before she joined the U.S. Attorney's Office.

When Barbara returned, I conveyed Elliot's message.

"Where is it showing," she asked.

I told her.

"It must show something other than raw sex. Elliot knows better than to lure me into an adult theatre."

"He was certain you would be interested."

---

"Oh, my god, it's Elliot's old girlfriend," Barbara whispered as the film opened with an Asian woman walking toward the camera wearing only high heels and a fur coat fully opened in the front.

I said, "Who knew her body looked like that?"

"Elliot, obviously."

We stayed for the show. Elliot's former lover challenged the Kama Sutra's number of sexual positions, with several partners. The thin plot was grossly forgettable.

We called Elliot when we got home. I only listened in and laughed along.

Barbara said, "You could have just told us she starred in a sex show."

"That would not have had the same impact. Weren't you shocked when a woman you know walked her naked body right up to the camera on the big screen?"

"I didn't know her that well."

"You knew she was sleeping with me."

"Did she teach you all those tricks, or did you teach her?"

"I bought her that fur coat. I may sue the producer. They didn't get my permission to use my coat in their dirty movie."

"So, you're saying you didn't give her that coat, you only loaned it to her. Do you plan to loan it to someone else?"

"No. But I could sell it."

"She certainly seemed to be enjoying herself."

"Screw Magazine gave her a high rating on their Peter Meter. Said something like, 'what she lacks in beauty she makes up for in enthusiasm.'"

"Who could argue with that?"

# CHAPTER FOURTEEN
## *Shared Secrets*

Miss Rowan took her duty to keep her legal work confidential very seriously. She seldom told me anything about her cases even during those years when we both worked for the Department of Justice. There were a few exceptions.

One day she came home smiling brightly, eager to share her joy. "I argued before a rabbinical court today."

"How did that happen?"

"You know that stuff I was studying last night?"

"No. I didn't read it, but I did see you cramming."

"Well, I have this witness in a fraud case who testified before the grand jury. Later, he came to see me. He said he couldn't testify at trial because he would get thrown out of his synagogue."

"Why?"

"That's what I asked him. He said his rabbi told him that if a Jew testified against another Jew, it would violate the Ninth Commandment."

"Don't make me look it up."

"Oh. The Ninth Commandment says not to bear false witness."

"I am sure you didn't ask the witness to lie."

"Of course not. I did ask him if he could arrange a meeting with his rabbi so I could try to clear up any misconceptions. He agreed. He wanted to testify against the criminal, but he also didn't want to get excommunicated."

"So?"

"So, I talked to Judge Weinfeld. He is a Talmudic scholar. I asked if he had ever heard of such an odd opinion. Not only had he heard of it, but he had also written that thick opinion I was trying to memorize last night."

"Aha."

"When I got to the synagogue to talk to the rabbi, I was escorted into a court room. There were four rabbis sitting behind an elevated bench, and a single folding chair facing them. One of them said, 'It is not our custom to shake hands. We hope you are not offended.' I said I understood, and I was not offended."

"I think I know why…"

"That's not the funny part. I sat down before them and explained the position that the United States was taking in the matter of the Ninth Commandment. Then they began to deliberate in Yiddish about what I had said in English. One of them misquoted me so I politely interrupted and explained that point in Yiddish. You should have seen their faces. I thought their eyeballs might roll down their cheeks. I had to bite my lips to keep from laughing. They were frozen, like statues. After a delightful pause, I said, 'Would you gentlemen like me to wait outside while you discuss this?' One of them asked, 'Do you speak Hebrew?' I said I didn't, so they immediately resumed their debate in Hebrew."

"Did you win?"

"Of course."

"How come you speak Yiddish?"

"I'm a New Yorker," she said as though all New Yorkers speak Yiddish.

Thirty years later, I recalled her comment when America's first Black Secretary of State, Colin Powell, surprised the Israeli delegation by speaking to them in fluent Yiddish. Secretary Powell was also a New Yorker. And like Barbara he succumbed with Covid-19.

# CHAPTER FIFTEEN

# *Cutting the Cord*

"When I leave the U.S. Attorney's office, I want to have an office like this one." Barbara's gaze swung around the light airy room and back to the big windows. "Assistant United States Attorneys seldom stay around long enough to retire."

I asked, "Did you see the wood-paneled office at the other end of the suite?"

"I liked the bookshelves in there, but the room is too dark."

We were visiting a housewarming at a four-room law office near the federal courthouse.

More about this office space later.

---

"I have finished my commitment to the U.S. Attorney, so I'm considering a job offer," Barbara told me.

"Where?"

"Here in Manhattan."

"Which law firm?"

"Not a law firm." She named one of America's top five pharmaceutical manufacturing companies. Let's just call it BigFive.

"How did they find you?

"I don't know. I was the Foreign Trademark Coordinator for Richardson-Merrell when I was in law school, maybe they heard about ..."

"So, you already know how to do the job."

"Oh no. I'm not going back to that. I'm a litigator. I'm sure they have plenty of trial cases."

"Big bucks? Big office?"

"I don't know, yet. I've got an interview next week. I just wanted to let you know. You aren't investigating BigFive, are you?"

"No ma'am."

---

"Hey, Harry, it's been quite a while since we last talked." The caller was a former FBI agent I had not seen for some time. I'll call him "John Smith," although that is not his name.

"What can I do for you, John?"

"You can stop by my office. I've got a proposal for you."

FBI agents who investigate crimes against corporations get job offers from time to time. I was used to it.

"Where's your office?"

"BigFive Corporate Headquarters." He gave me the address.

I wondered if he was doing a background on my wife, rather than trying to recruit me, or perhaps both.

I said, "I have a one o'clock meeting not far from there. I could drop in around two."

"Excellent. The guards in the lobby will bring you right up."

They did indeed. I was treated like visiting royalty.

"How do you like my office, Harry?"

"A corner office with great views, who could ask for anything more?"

"It could be yours."

"Oh?"

"Yeah. I've been promoted to Human Resources Director, so my first task is to replace myself as Security Director."

"Would I get this fancy office?"

"Yes. But not my secretary. She goes with me. Just down the hall. This is the executive floor."

"I guess you know who my wife is."

"No. Should I?"

"She's an Assistant U.S. Attorney."

"Great! If we ever need to refer a case to the U.S. Attorney, you have a connection there."

"Since the insurance companies started to require Wall Street firms to have security directors, I've noticed that most of them spend their days scheduling the uniformed guards from basement offices. You don't fit that mold."

"Absolutely not. We've had a security director for a long time, longer than I've been here. And I have a deputy who manages the guards."

"What do you do? What does the job entail?"

"Whatever you want it to."

"Really?"

"The board of directors have no idea what a security director should be doing. For example, my predecessor was a retired police captain. He spent most of his time on liaison with the NYPD. Lots of luncheons, retirement parties, stuff like that."

"Sounds like a lot of eating."

"I like to travel. We have operations on every continent, except Antarctica. I have visited most of them. First Class, of course."

"Amazing."

"You can do whatever you want so long as you can justify it to the board. You can make this job whatever you want it to be."

"I have a wife…"

"Me too. I didn't take her on many of my over-seas inspection tours. She doesn't like to travel as much as I do. But whenever there was a conference involved, she came along."

"I was about to say, 'I need to talk to my wife about your offer.'"

"Of course. Tell her we will pay you three times what you are making now."

"How much?"

"I don't know, exactly. How much is the Bureau paying you?"

"Let me get back to you."

"Call me tomorrow."

"I will."

"Good."

---

"As a professional investigator, I don't believe in coincidences, Barbara, but this offer looks legit, and we could wind up working together, again."

"As the fates would have it, their legal department called and rescheduled my meeting. I'll be sitting down with them in the morning."

"Fates? You believe in fates?"

"No. I'm more suspicious about this than you are."

"I'll call John and tell him that I can't give him an answer till the day-after-tomorrow."

---

"Hey, honey. I'm calling because I know you're eager to learn how my meeting went."

"So, you are now in charge of litigation for BigFive Pharmaceuticals?"

"Quite the contrary."

"Oh."

"They keep their lawyers in cubicles with a ten-minute break in the morning and another in the afternoon when the coffee cart comes by and rings a little bell. There is not enough money on earth to make me want to work there."

"And who could blame you?"

"You could. I hope this doesn't spoil the bigtime offer you have pending with BigFive."

"Not to worry. My main interest was the fact that you would be working there. You know I love the Bureau a lot more than I hate it."

"So, you're gonna tell BigFive 'No?'"

"The sooner the better. I don't want to leave John in suspense."

———————

"Hey, John. Sorry to do this to you, but I'm gonna have to decline your offer."

"Mind if I ask why?"

"Family reasons."

"Okay if I write you a letter saying you have many sterling qualities, but we have decided on someone else?"

"I won't even ask why you would do that, but I don't mind."

"That way it looks like I'm the one who broke the engagement, and there is nothing wrong with BigFive."

"Nothing wrong with BigFive so far as I know. Want a letter from me stating that?"

"No. Let me do the letter writing. Sorry I won't have you down the hall, Harry."

"Me too."

---

"Harry, remember that law office open house we attended. That office I liked?"

"Yeah."

"That office suite is available. I'm gonna ask Elliot if he would like to share office space with me, again."

"Here's what I don't understand, Barbara. Everyone praised your work at the U.S. Attorney's office. How come the other assistants get scooped up by big law firms, but you didn't even get an interview? Just pure racism?"

"It may be racism, but it's not pure."

"Not pure? What's the impurity?"

"Gender discrimination. Right now, there is a class action lawsuit brought by women lawyers against ten New York law firms for not giving female applicants a fair shake."

"Are you one of them?"

"No. I don't have time for that. I'm still busy trying to make a living."

"You make more money than I do."

"I'm gonna have to borrow money to set up my new office."

"How much."

"Five thousand dollars."

"Wish I had it. I'd give it to you."

"I know. I'm borrowing it from Matty. We've drawn up a loan agreement, with a repayment schedule, and more interest than the bank is giving him."

"Did Elliot ante up?"

"Of course. He wants that dark paneled office in the back. Calls it 'the fee-setting room.'"

"It is impressive."

"Elliot's has already made deals with TV network reporters to rent them his office from time to time for their interviews of important witnesses in stories about legal matters."

"He seems to be a sharp businessman."

"He is."

"Barbara, where did you find the little secretary in the micro-mini-skirt, and high-heeled, thigh-high boots?"

"How did you happen to notice her bare thighs, Harry? Did you look under her desk?"

"No, *Bootsy* was standing up when I came in."

"I hope she didn't bend over."

"No. She was coming out of that little office over by Elliot's fee-setting room."

"That's gonna be Stuart's office."

"Stuart?"

"He writes appeals. I can't wait for you to meet him. He's got the cutest little girl. And he spends a lot of time with her. Takes her to museums, to Central Park, shopping at Zabar's, even here."

"Did he bring Bootsy with him?"

"No. Elliot and I hired her. Wish I could tell her how to dress."

"Why not? You're her boss."

"But I'm not her mother. Elliot thinks her fashionable outfits will let clients know we are keeping up with the times. I would prefer a more conservative image."

"Where did you get the Chinese desk?"

"That was in my old office in the village. Eliot has been keeping it for me. Oh. Speaking of things Chinese, here's my new client, Jimmy. He owns Chinese restaurants. Jimmy, this is my husband, Harry. He's just leaving."

The diminutive man in an expensive suit smiled at me and shook my hand. "Hello, Mr. Rowan."

I noticed the Rolex watch and big diamond ring on his other hand.

He turned to Barbara. "What you need are benches in the hall."

"Why?"

"I will refer immigrants to you. And I will get you some people to fill out their forms. You get a hundred dollars for each form. All you have to do is sign."

"I'm not an immigration lawyer."

"You're smart. You could learn. All they do is sign forms."

"Jimmy, I don't want to be McDonald's. I want to be The Four Seasons."

"McDonald's makes a lot more money than The Four Seasons."

"Why don't you sit down here, Jimmy? My husband has to go now." She looked at me and nodded toward the door.

I gave her a grin. "Since you can't go to lunch with me, is it okay if I ask Bootsy?"

She smirked right back at me. "Don't you dare."

---

"Sorry if I'm grumpy tonight, Harry. It's not you. It's an old man who was a client of my father's accounting firm in Harlem."

"What did he do?"

"My daddy was what we called a 'race man.' That means whenever possible we did business with Black people."

"Uh huh."

"Growing up, my doctor, my dentist, my ballet instructors… White professionals didn't make Black people feel welcome. Daddy's clients were mostly Black-owned businesses."

"Like the guy who made you mad."

"Right. When he walked into my office, I assumed he was going to retain me. I asked him what his legal problem was. He said, 'Oh no, sweetheart. This is an important matter, a federal criminal case. I understand you have a Jewish lawyer here. I want to see him.'"

"Federal criminal cases are all you have been handling for the last four years."

"Exactly. I don't think Elliot has ever been in the federal courthouse."

"What did you say?"

"I said, 'Right this way. The Jewish lawyer is down this hall in the Important Matters Office. I'll introduce you.'"

"Did he retain Elliot?"

"I don't know. I went back to my office, locked the door, and stomped my feet. I didn't scream. Aloud."

"With any luck, Elliot will charge him plenty. You'll feel better when you learn the old man got convicted and sent to prison."

"I don't want anything about him to enter my head ever again."

"Let's talk about something else."

"Okay."

---

"Would you like to go to Jamaica, Harry."

"Of course."

"Matty and Eileen want to celebrate my return to private practice with a trip to Jamaica."

"Don't you owe them five grand?"

"Not anymore."

"Since we have separate bank accounts, how much will I have to pony up?"

"I'll let you know. We're going to Port Antonio. That's where my daddy came from."

---

"Barbara, you are not going to believe this."

"You've never lied to me. What happened?

"I had lunch with Robin Moore. He was telling me he took Eddie Egan to Jamaica to debrief him for the stories in The French Connection."

"Hmmm."

"I told him we might be going there. He asked where we planned to stay. I told him Port Antonio and he was delighted. He owns a house in Port Antonio. He suggested we stay at his house."

"You think that's a good idea?"

"No. So, I said your dad was from Port Antonio and let him believe we will be staying with relatives."

---

"How come there's a lock on the refrigerator?" Matty asked the housekeeper.

Her given name began with the letter "I" and she was tiny, so we called her "Little Aye."

"Because I am responsible for the food and drink," she told Matty.

He asked, "What if I want a beer in the middle of the night?"

"Wake me," she said.

"We could get a few beers out before her bedtime," I said to Matty.

"You drink warm beer? What are you, British?"

"I'm a light sleeper," said Little Aye. "Feel free to wake me anytime."

Barbara assured her, "We will try to put the boys to bed at a decent hour."

"Yeah," said Eileen. "We don't want to disturb the next-door neighbors. Their house is only five or ten feet away."

"There is no one there," said the housekeeper. "Mr. Moore doesn't come here often."

"Robin Moore?" I asked.

"Yes, the famous author."

"Oh, crap," Barbara and I said in unison.

"What?" asked Matty and Eileen.

―――――――――

"I don't want one of those sausages you bought yesterday," said Barbara. "They didn't smell quite right to me."

"I told Little Aye to cook them thoroughly," I said. "Whatever germs were in there are dead now."

Eileen said, "I'm with Barbara. I'm not eating one of those."

"That leaves more for Harry and me," said Matty.

Barbara's keen nose and Eileen's good judgement were vindicated within the hour. I got so sick that I didn't go out that day.

———

"How are you doing, sweetheart?"

"I'm better now, Barbara. Where's Matty and Eileen?"

"They're still limbo dancing. Well, Matty is limbo dancing. There is a limit to how low Eileen will go."

"How low did you go?"

"You know me better than that. Oh. Here she comes now. Where's Matty, Eileen?"

"He locked himself in the men's room till I get back with a fresh pair of pants, and shorts."

"What happened?"

"He had a belated sausage attack. Right under the limbo bar."

"Did anybody notice?" asked Barbara.

"Everybody. They were all laughing."

"Oh, you poor woman," said Barbara.

Once Eileen was out of earshot, my wife said, "Please don't ever embarrass me in public, Harry. I would just die."

———

"So, you guys are here in Jamaica for the cricket test matches, eh?" Matty asked four British bookies who had asked us for directions back to Kingston.

"Right," one of them said. "It's rather like your world series of baseball."

"It's being played here in Jamaica?" Eileen asked.

The big blond British blokes all nodded, and one said, "It's England against the West Indies cricket team."

Barbara said, "Since you have wandered across the entire island, the least we can do is offer you a beer."

We all gathered around our table and drank beer while Barbara plotted a route for their return trip. She loved maps.

During the conversation, one of the bookies mentioned that he and his pals shared a favorite sport: beating up Pakistani guys. They used a derogatory term for that practice which I will not repeat.

"What the hell is that?" I asked.

One of them said, "You find a Pakistani and thrash him soundly."

Another said, "His mum's a judge. She always gets us out of jail if we get arrested."

Matty said, "It doesn't seem very sporting, beating a smaller, non-violent, person."

"Oh, they can be quite evil when you've bashed them about a bit."

I could see Barbara's eyes flashing up at the bookies and down at the map, where she was erasing and replotting vigorously.

When the bookies left, Barbara said, "I don't think they will get back to Kingston in time to take any bets."

"How far is it?"

"The route I gave them will be a tour of the entire island, with two loops through cockpit country."

# CHAPTER SIXTEEN

# *Private Practice*

"Any chance you could take an hour off tomorrow, Harry?"

"Unless something comes up, I don't see why not."

"Good. I want you to carry my revolver down to the police headquarters for me."

"Why?"

"I applied for a pistol permit, and they turned me down because Elliot has one."

"What? Walk me through that again."

"I want a pistol permit, so I copied Elliot's application. The two reasons he gave for needing one were that clients may sometimes pay in cash, and the cash has to be carried to the bank, and sometimes potential witnesses must be interviewed in dangerous neighborhoods at night."

"You could call me."

"Don't let the NYPD hear you say that. They rejected my application because they noted that there is a man in my office who has a carry permit, so I could ask him to accompany me whenever I felt unsafe."

"You're kidding. They put that in writing?"

"Yes, they did. So, I sued them for gender discrimination. The court ordered them to give me a permit. They require me to bring in the gun I'd like to carry so they can check it out."

"Tomorrow?"

"Right. I'm afraid that they will arrest me on the spot for carrying it in without a permit."

"Thanks for inviting me. I want to see this dog and pony show."

---

"Are you the officer I should see about my pistol permit?"

"And you are?"

"Barbara Ann Rowan."

As he rummaged through the stack of papers on his desk, the bored police officer asked, "Did you bring the pistol with you?"

"Give it to him, Harry."

I handed the unloaded revolver to the policeman, with the cylinder open.

He looked closely at the serial number and jotted it down before he handed Barbara her permit and gave her weapon back to me.

He told Barbara, "Don't load that gun until you are out of the building."

"Don't you want to see if I know how to load it safely?"

"No. Just go."

"Thank you, officer."

I walked Barbara back to her office where she loaded her favorite firearm.

She said, "To get a driver's license, you have to take a written test about the traffic laws, and you have to drive an officer around to demonstrate that you know how to handle a car."

I laughed.

She shook her head. "He didn't even want to see if I could load my gun, let alone demonstrate any basic grasp of pertinent laws, or the ability to handle it safely."

"He didn't write the regulations, honey."

"If he did, Black women would be prohibited from carrying pistols."

"He didn't write your rejection letter, either. You have no idea what that policeman may think about these issues."

"I was amazed that he didn't ask you what legal right you had to tote my gun."

"I was surprised that after he handed you your permit, he passed your pistol back to me."

---

One day I stopped by my wife's office at noon to see if she was available for lunch. She wasn't but she had a gift for me.

"That government credential case you carry around is starting to fall apart, so I got you a nice new leather one. Here."

"Hmm. It looks just like my old one, but it feels way better."

She dropped my ragged old credential case in her middle desk drawer.

A few days later she came home with a great story to tell.

"Do you know agent (I don't recall his name)?"

"There are eleven hundred agents in the office. I don't think I know that one."

"I don't think you do, either, or he wouldn't have made such an ass of himself."

"What did he do?"

"He stormed into my office, right past Bootsy, flashed his creds and said, 'You represent Cuba [pronounced Koo Buh] and you are going to tell me where he is.'

"I said, 'I have represented more than one individual called Cuba. Why should I help you?'

"'Because I have a warrant for his arrest and I'm going to arrest you for harboring a fugitive if you don't tell me where to find him right now.'

"I said, 'Are you sure you're an FBI agent. May I see those credentials, again, please?'

He stuck them right in my face. I took them out of his hand, laid them on my lap, and pretended to study them. I switched them with your old credential case, and said, 'With your attitude, I don't think you should be representing the Federal Bureau of Investigation.'

I tossed the empty case into my shredder and turned it on. I thought he was going to have a heart attack. He couldn't get his words together. So, before he peed his pants, I tossed him his creds and said, 'Get out of my office.'"

---

"Is my tie straight?" I asked Barbara.

"I hate cocktail parties," she said.

"So why are we going?"

"It's expected of everyone in the legal community. Colleagues would be insulted if I turned them down."

"I find it enormously entertaining."

"You would. You don't seem to feel they are judging you, looking for a flaw."

"Quite the contrary. They expect a blue-eyed, blond, FBI agent to be some sort of neo-Nazi. But when they talk to you, the Chair of the New York State Bar Civil Rights Committee, they expect a bleeding-heart liberal. They have our political position reversed."

"Come on. Neither of us are radicals. I'm just a little right of center and you're a little left."

"Yeah, but that is not what is expected of us."

"We can't fix stupid."

---

"Damn! Barbara, when you said you were helping arrange this judicial conference in Puerto Rico, I thought I could show you around the island. Now I find this resort doesn't have rental cars."

"It may be just as well, there are plenty of complaints I have to deal with. I can't wander too far off the plantation."

"We are sort of trapped here. The management can't understand why anyone would want to leave and visit the real Puerto Rico when everything your heart desires is right here."

"I'll tell you what's not *right here*, Jack Daniels.'

"I noticed that."

"Well, one of the judges can't imagine not having a shot of Jack Daniels after dinner."

"Hey! That's our ticket out of here. They've got to give us a ride."

A few hours later, we walked into a small liquor store in the mountain town of Yabucoa and I said, in

Spanish, "I'll take two bottles of Jack Daniels Old Number 7."

The half-dozen people in the store stared at me like deer in the headlights.

I asked Barbara, in English, "Is my Spanish that bad?"

She said, "No. Just your manners." Then she announced in Spanish, "Please excuse us. We'll be right back." She marched me outside and said, "This time, greet them properly. I'm sure you know how."

"Oh, Lord. I had forgotten we are not in New York."

Our encore entrance was much more pleasant. In Spanish, I told the man behind the counter how beautiful his island home was, particularly the mountains. I asked him how his family was doing, as though we were old friends. We chatted about the weather and world politics for a while before I casually mentioned that I, and an important friend, both liked Jack Daniels Old Number 7.

He allowed as how he happened to have two bottles. Would I like them?

"That would be ever so nice."

Back at the beach resort we made one federal judge very happy.

Later, Barbara told me, "The second circuit judges from the mainland were shocked to learn that the federal judges here in Puerto Rico carry pistols."

"Well, not too long ago, the chief of police was shot to death on the steps of the cathedral, right after a church service."

"I suggested the New York judges might consider arming themselves."

"What did they say?"

"Most disagreed with me, so I told them I have a pistol permit in New York. You should have seen their faces."

"Did they think of you as a criminal?"

"I don't know. But their reaction made me feel like a delicate flower. They were so stunned that a woman would carry a gun."

---

Back in Harlem, we delivered Clara's groceries, as usual, one Saturday morning.

"Mom, what are you doing on the floor?" Barbara asked.

Clara said, "I tripped on the rug and couldn't get up."

I said, "You have the phone down there, why didn't you call us?"

"You two are so busy. I didn't want to bother you. I was chatting with my friends. I could have asked them for help, but I knew you two were coming this morning."

Barbara asked, "How long have you been lying there?"

"Just yesterday and today. I knew you were bringing my groceries so I …"

"Mother! This will never do. You have to move in with us."

I said, "We have a new apartment with two master bedrooms, each with its own bathroom. We rented it with you in mind."

Barbara said, "The building belongs to the Guggenheim, just across Fifth Avenue from Central Park. It's right on the block with The Dalton School. You know where that is."

"I don't want to intrude in your marriage. You two seem so happy."

"How can we be happy worrying about you crawling around on the floor?"

Thus, Clara came to live with us, for a decade, until she passed away.

# CHAPTER SEVENTEEN
## *Dog Days*

"Hey Baby, let me introduce you to Loco."

The tiny Yorkshire Terrier I led into our apartment looked like a rat on a string.

"What a sweet little puppy. Why did you name her 'Loco'?"

"I didn't. She was already named, but we can call her anything you like."

For a few weeks Clara and Loco gave one another company all day while Barbara and I were working.

One evening, Barbara said, "Harry, the vet says if we don't breed Loco, or have her spayed, she'll get mean."

"She's been cutting her teeth on your bookcase and my bar. Let's get her spayed."

What a terrible mistake that was. Loco didn't survive the surgery.

"Harry, could you stop by the vet's place and pick up Loco's leash and collar? I can't do that without crying in public."

"What about her body?"

"What about it?"

"Shouldn't we bury it somewhere?"

"Where?"

"Maybe Central Park. She loved Central Park."

"You can't dig holes in Central Park. Let the vet take care of it. He killed her."

"You know it was the anesthesia, sweetheart. She was so little they accidentally overdosed her."

I had two very unhappy women at home. Each time I noticed Loco's little toothmarks on something, I felt sad, too.

There was nothing for it, I had to get another yorkie. Her name was Midget. We never changed it. Well, we called her Midgi most of the time.

We didn't take her to the veterinarian who lost Loco. However, her vet gave us the same choice: have her neutered, bred, or live with an angry dog.

This time we chose to have an additional little yorkie or two. Or so we thought.

Midget was bigger and calmer than Loco had been. She ran a mile and a half with me every morning around the Central Park Reservoir Track until pregnancy swelled her so much that she got cinders in her stomach fur, and on her tongue from panting. She still wanted to go, but we couldn't let her.

Due to Barbara's body build, she would never jog in public. So, I had to jog alone, again.

We took turns walking Midgi around the block. We bought a long-handled pooper scooper to pick up her droppings and bag them.

One day Barbara came home laughing. "A man was walking with his little boy, and they saw me scooping the poop. He said to his son, 'That's why you can't have a dog. You would have to clean up after it.' I said to Midgi, 'That's why you can't have a little boy. They're too lazy to take care of a dog.'"

"Did they laugh?"

"The little boy did."

I was in an FBI garage just four blocks from home when I called for my messages. I had an urgent message from Barbara, so I called her immediately.

"Harry! Harry! Can you come home? Midgi's having her puppies."

"Puppies? Not one but two?"

"No. She's had four so far and they just keep coming. I could use some help."

I hopped into an FBI car and told my partner where I lived. He turned on the siren. We slid to a stop in front of my building. I ran past the doorman and up the stairs to the second floor. No time to wait for an elevator.

"I think she's through," Barbara said.

Midget lay like a wet rag on the floor, gasping for air.

Barbara had delivered seven puppies, one of them stillborn. Every one of them small enough to hide in your hand.

I said, "I'm glad she doesn't have to do this again."

Caring for our miniscule charges was more of a joy than a chore. Midget couldn't nurse all of them, so we fed them with an eyedropper. It wasn't long until they developed recognizable personalities.

We named the biggest one Finbarr after Sergeant Finbarr Devine, who led the New York City Police Department's Emerald Society Pipes and Drums. His brother was an FBI agent I worked with. Finding a family to adopt Finbarr was no problem.

The smallest puppy, and the only female, was Yorkshire Pudding, better known as Pudi.

One who turned out to be near sighted we named Henry J. Friendly, after a federal judge, who was not amused. We called his namesake, "Mr. Friendly."

Barnaby was born with a misaligned frame, so it took him a long time to learn to walk, more sideways than forward. When he was big enough to take out for a walk, he would fall on his side trying to kick a fireplug along with his brothers. This challenged pup made a Catholic nun very happy.

I don't recall the names of the other two, because they were promptly adopted by friends, who were delighted to get free pets.

––––––––

"Get away from that bum!" Barbara barked at our herd of yorkies. Pound for pound they could pull harder on a leash than a Caterpillar tractor. "Don't let him touch you. You don't know where his hands have been."

The man lying on the park bench across the street from the Guggenheim Museum said, "I ain't gonna hurt you dogs, lady." He took a drink from his jug of wine.

"Disgusting!" Barbara said of the guy in the slouch hat and ragged overcoat as she pulled her puppies away.

The dogs couldn't be fooled, however. They knew it was me in disguise, drinking black coffee from a wine bottle.

Terrorists had been breaking into museums and vandalizing them. The case agent had identified their pattern and correctly guessed they would hit one that night. I volunteered to cover the Guggenheim, since I lived next door.

Several friends and neighbors had walked right by me, but not our little guys. They almost blew my cover.

# CHAPTER EIGHTEEN
## *The Big Move*

Barbara said, "I need a break, Harry."

"You have been working long hours."

"Yeah. I've been representing gangsters. They pay well, but they expect me to meet their families, particularly their mothers, and go to family functions."

"Family functions?"

"Funerals, wedding, christenings, and stuff like that."

"Funerals?"

"None of my clients have been wacked, yet. But one of their brothers was. All the women wore black, did a lot of loud weeping, and kept looking at me because I didn't."

"So, you're not cut out to be a gangland mouthpiece, eh?"

"I keep telling them they can hire my legal talent, but not my friendship. They don't understand the difference."

"Time for you to go job hunting, baby. There's lots of lucrative things you can do."

"I prefer to do pro bono work but we're not rich enough for me to do that full time."

"You mean like representing that orphans' home in Harlem?"

"Yeah. I spend about half my time on stuff like that."

"So, if I made more money, you could devote all your energy to humanitarian efforts."

"Don't blame yourself, Harry. It's not your fault that I like to be on the side of the angels."

"If I got transferred to the boondocks, we could afford to live on my salary."

"I've only lived in Manhattan and Europe. I'm not sure I'm ready for middle America."

"I'm not sure they're ready for you."

---

"You're not going to believe this, Harry."

"Try me."

"You know we were talking about moving yesterday."

"I know I was."

"We got a job offer today. Working for the government. We'd have to move."

"They're not trying to make you the U.S. Attorney in Panama, again, are they."

"No. The Bureau refused to transfer you to Panama. But this job offer is for both of us."

"Tell me more."

"John Nields called."

John Nields had studied at The Dalton School while Barbara was a student there. They were also Assistant United States Attorneys in the Southern District of New York at the same time. And he and his wife Gail were our neighbors.

"What's John up to?" I asked.

"He's in charge of a Congressional investigation of the South Korean government bribing members of the House."

"What makes you think the Bureau will let me work on that?"

"John's pretty confident he can get them to lend you to the committee."

"Tell him I'd love to investigate corrupt congressmen."

A few days later I was ordered to report to Washington to turn in my badge, gun, and manuals because I was being assigned to the House of Representatives. I knew FBI agents who had been loaned to Congress before, so it wasn't unprecedented.

Due to the notoriety of the Watergate burglary investigation that caused President Ricard Nixon to resign two years earlier, our inquiry was labeled "Koreagate" by the press.

We worked for the Committee on Standards of Official Conduct, which the media called "the Ethics Committee."

The Chairman referred to Barbara and me as "the odd couple." Interracial marriages were still remarkable.

Barbara called Congress "the last plantation," because all the federal laws they had passed to protect workers exempted themselves. (That has since changed.)

We were required to take typing tests, but not because our jobs involved typing anything. We had secretaries in those days who took dictation. However, one powerful congressman's secretary, Elizabeth Ray, had written a book entitled *The Washington Fringe Benefit* in which she said, "I can't type, I can't file, I can't even answer the phone." Although she was on the payroll of a committee run by her boss as a clerk-secretary, her real job was to provide him sexual favors. She didn't even go to the office. After her book was published, he resigned, and all job applicants thereafter had to take typing tests.

Barbara shared an office with two other lawyers. Just down the hall, I was housed with two investigators, one on loan from the Drug Enforcement Administration and the other from DC Legal Aid.

"Here's a good trick," I told her. "When you interview a member of congress, get their state wrong. It really shakes them up, makes them feel less important, and focuses their attention on your questions."

"I can't do that, sweetheart. It would make me look uninformed."

"People love to explain themselves to the uninformed."

While Barbara sparred with heavyweight law firms that represented powerful members of Congress, I interviewed witnesses wherever they might be found. Traveling with another investigator, I went to Athens, Greece; Geneva, Switzerland; Monroe, Louisiana; Los Angeles, California; etc.

Meanwhile, Clara took care of Midgi, Pudi, and Mr. Friendly in our split-level house in the woods in Prince William County, Virginia.

"I worry about them wandering off," she said.

"They're not going anywhere," Barbara told her. "They're city dogs. They walk around the pool and the garden, but they only step off the paved path to do their business, just like they hopped off the curbs in New York."

I said, "They bark at the squirrels and deer and the other critters, but they don't go after them. They are not comfortable with their feet on grass. And they are certainly not going into the woods."

Clara also had to take spam calls for Mr. Friendly. That's right. Our dog had a phone. Actually, he had our only phone.

When we moved, I had said, "I think this is extortion. The phone company charges extra for an unlisted number. They aren't doing more. They are charging us more to do less. It's as though they are saying, *Here's the deal, buddy. You pay us a little extra each month or we will put your name, address, and phone number in a book and give it to all those folks you've arrested. You wouldn't want anything bad to happen to you, or your family, eh?"*

Barbara said, "I don't want it in my name either."

Clara said, "You can put it in any name you want."

She may have been suggesting we list the phone to her, but her daughter said, "How about Henry J. Friendly? He lives here."

And thus, we enjoyed daily humorous encounters with telephone solicitors, who were real live human beings in those days.

"May I speak with Mr. Friendly?"

"He's not in right now. He's out in the backyard watering a tree."

Mr. Friendly also got junk mail. A letter from a major insurance company said they were looking for a reliable representative in our area and asked if Mr. Friendly could recommend someone.

He could. And he did. He recommended a dog who lived nearby. Let's call her "Judy Jones." We returned the insurance company's form in their postage-paid, self-addressed envelope.

Apparently, they didn't take note of the paw-print signature. They called Judy Jones's house. We had put her human companions on notice, so they were delighted to tell the caller that Judy was unavailable, having fallen asleep on the kitchen floor after wolfing down her dinner. The insurance company didn't call back.

Mr. Friendly even got a preapproved MasterCard. His credit record was pure. I suggested we put his paw print on that too. Barbara explained how that might constitute a crime. So, on advice of counsel, I did not pursue that path to easy money.

We owned the tall wooden fence between our backyard and the next-door neighbors. They hung rabbit hutches on their side of our fence. We didn't mind.

Pudi was the only pup small enough to get under the fence. She went next door and barked at the rabbits on more than one occasion. The German immigrant woman thought the tiny terrier was cute.

One Saturday morning, Pudi came crawling back under the fence clutching the back of a rabbit's neck in her teeth. She dragged the bunny through the dirt into our yard.

Barbara tried mouth-to-nose resuscitation while I massaged its chest, but the white rabbit was dead.

We took it inside, shampooed and rinsed the dirt out of its fur, and dried it with a blow dryer. I climbed over the fence and carefully put the carcass back into its little home, surrounded by the other rabbit hutches.

An hour or so later, a spine-chilling shriek got me back up on the fence. The neighbor was holding the dead bunny and babbling in German.

I asked, "What happened?"

"Hans! Hans! My rabbit! My rabbit!"

"Oh, my. Your bunny died."

"He died yesterday! I buried him in the yard! But he got back in his cage!"

"Wow! That's remarkable."

She is probably still telling the story of the miraculous resurrection of Hans the Hare.

Barbara said, "We thought we were aiding and abetting a murderer, but we were only aiding and abetting a grave robber."

---

Barbara and I played Clara's books-for-the-blind as we commuted. The three of us discussed those classic stories after we sent the cassettes back to the Library of Congress.

Our lovely neighbor, Regina, an avid reader, sometimes joined our discussions. She visited Clara every day and made sure she was alright.

---

"Look at these letters, Harry." Barbara had just opened her mail at home. "First, I have to tell you that I sent my pistol permit back to the NYPD. I explained that I had moved to Virginia and wouldn't be carrying a gun in New York anymore."

I read the first letter. "Holy crap!" The General Counsel for the City of New York had informed the Attorney General of Virginia that an armed woman had moved to his state. It gave him her address but did not indicate a copy for her.

The second one was a reply, with a copy for Barbara, attaching a photocopy of the letter from New York. Virginia's top law enforcement officer informed his New York City counterpart that "Virginia has been welcoming armed women for nearly 400 years."

# CHAPTER NINETEEN
# *The Federal Trade Commission*

"See that wrap-around third-floor balcony? That's mine," Barbara said.

"Wow! You're at the point of the Federal Triangle, looking down at this fountain."

"And looking straight across at the Capitol Building."

The light changed and I turned around the apex of the massive limestone building onto Pennsylvania Avenue.

"Take a left on Seventh Street and I'll show you my own personal parking spot in the basement."

"I don't know when you will need it, since I'm gonna drop you off every day on my way to Buzzard Point."

"Well, whenever you're out of town, I won't have to look for a parking garage around here."

Barbara was much more open with me about her work as Assistant Director of the FTC in charge of the Bureau of Consumer Protection. We discussed her management issues in generic terms almost every day. Nothing about legal strategies or anything proprietary.

My first exposure to her new office was on a Saturday.

I said, "The morning light through that wall of windows is fabulous!"

"That's true, Harry, but it illuminates how dirty this room is."

"How many people will be working with you in here?"

"Just me. I told the building manager that my office is filthy, and she sent me a vacuum cleaner."

"How did you deal with that?"

"I have scheduled a meeting with her for Monday morning. I'll pretend she was joking."

"This wall should be in the Smithsonian."

"What do you mean?"

"You have a historic collection of phone lines, starting with this ancient one, solid copper wire wrapped in woven cotton. It seems they cut each old wire and stapled the next generation on the wall above it."

"You mean those wires could be removed?"

"I can rip them off right now. The staple holes will have to be spackled."

"I can do that. But what about my phone?"

"Your phone is hooked up to this fat cable on the floor. You have several lines."

"While we are buying the spackle, I can buy wallpaper, so they don't paint my office walls battle-ship gray, again."

"I'm guessing you want to do that now."

"We can start today and if we don't get finished, we can come in tomorrow. Nobody works here on weekends."

---

"How was your first day, Barbara?"

"We had a management meeting. It was as White as the Vienna Boys Choir. There is one other woman."

"Is she White?"

"Of course."

"Were you uncomfortable?"

"No. Everyone was nice to me. Of course, I imagine some of them suppose I was only hired because I'm a triple statistic."

"Triple statistic?"

"Black. Female. Spanish speaker."

"How about the other languages you speak?"

"Those are not priority populations, right now."

"Did anyone ask about your background?"

"They didn't have to. When the Director introduced me, he said he hired me because he needed an experienced trial lawyer, and he mentioned my work for the House."

"Which do you think was more important to them?"

"Lots of corporations run right to Congress when the FTC proposes a new regulation that they don't like. So, I think my colleagues imagine I'm in tight with the law makers."

"Did you have your meeting with the building manager?

"I did."

"How did she like your new wallpaper?"

"She didn't seem to notice. I don't think she had ever been in that office before."

"Lucky we hauled off all those old wires."

"Yeah. But we left enough detritus for her to agree I needed a visit from the janitor. Regularly."

"Yay!"

"We have a retirement party after work on Wednesday, Harry. Think you could come? I'd like you to meet the people I work with."

"It's hard to schedule crime, baby, but I'll try my best."

---

"So, what do you think of my lawyers?"

"They're a very intellectual bunch. I'm sure they think I'm a neanderthal moron."

"Why?"

"I didn't know the washing instructions on clothes, or the contents listed on food containers, were all due to FTC regulations."

"I think they found you fascinating."

"They told you that?"

"No. But the way the women looked at you got my jealousy juices churning."

"You're kidding."

"Even a gay guy was following you around."

"He was trying to tell me about the proposed detergent rule. Apparently, the only difference between laundry soaps is labeling and advertising."

"Some of my attorneys have been working on that issue for years."

―――――――――

*"This is déjà vu all over again,"* I said to myself as I rolled toward the front door of the Federal Trade Commission one evening.

While waiting at a light, I had seen Barbara out by the curb talking to someone in a white Cadillac Coupe deVille. A few of her lawyers were ten or twelve paces behind her, watching.

As I drew near, the driver got out of the Cadillac. He was a middle-aged man in a gray business suit. He took handcuffs off his belt as he walked around his car.

I swooped in, popped out of our car, and rushed to Barbara, as manacle man approached her other side.

"Senior Detective," she said to him, "let me present my husband." She turned to me. "Special Agent Gossett, perhaps you can explain the civil rights laws to this long-time lawman."

I held up my credentials.

He gulped. "I am terribly sorry, ma'am. I must be getting old. I totally misunderstood."

"Even though he's off duty," Barbara told me, "This Senior Detective was thoughtful enough to stop and try to get a suspected prostitute off Pennsylvania Avenue."

He was backing away.

I said, "Gee, I've never seen a hooker with a briefcase before."

"Apparently he has. He even offered to give me a ride."

The Cadillac whooshed away.

The lawyers behind us buzzed excitedly, particularly the women, none of whom had ever been asked to "move it along."

"You got his name, right?"

"I did. He showed me his badge and even told me he is not a vice officer, and not on duty, just a concerned citizen."

"You gonna give me his name?"

"Absolutely not. Let's not go through that again."

"We owe him a civilian complaint. There are plenty of witnesses." I nodded toward the FTC lawyers. "Metropolitan Police Headquarters is just two blocks from here."

"You are my hero, but don't try to be my champion. This is my fight. You stay out of it."

"Okay. I'll let you pick my battles when it comes to racism. But feel free to put me in coach. I'm ready to rock."

———————

"Harry, I have created a monster. Or rather a monstrous situation," Barbara said as she climbed into the car for our drive home on another evening.

"Couldn't be too bad. You're laughing."

"It's just so silly. I've got a little redneck who didn't understand why the Black women were offended by the N-word."

"You're kidding.

"No, I'm not. The Black employees never brought it up before, but now that I'm there, they complained."

"And he was surprised?"

"*She* was amazed. She said everyone she knew, including all her relatives, use the N-word regularly."

"Where's she from?"

"La Plata, Maryland."

"Hmm."

"I told her she couldn't use that word at work, if she wanted to keep her job."

"What's monstrous about that?"

"Well, now she comes and confesses to me every time she lets slip the N-word."

"Did you ask her to tattle on herself?"

"No. And no one has complained again after that first wave."

"Sounds like she doesn't want you to hear about her misconduct from anyone else. Shows she's trying."

"I think the Black staffers were testing me. So now they probably think I condone her conduct."

"Ask them."

"Good idea."

———

"You're looking smug today, my darling," I said as Barbara got into our sedan after work.

"I fired a guy."

167

"What did he do?"

"It was for what he didn't do."

"What was that?"

"His assigned legal work."

"How did that go over?"

"Several division chiefs told me they recommended his requests for transfer to another division to get rid of him. He has done very little work in the years he's been here."

"Why didn't one of them fire him?"

"That's what I asked each of them. They said they didn't want to get involved with all the required paperwork. I told them they failed to do their jobs."

"Firing someone is not a pleasant duty."

"Neither is arresting people, but you do that all the time."

"So how did he take it?"

"He was offended. He said I wouldn't dare fire him because he would sue me."

"Let me guess what you said."

"Go ahead."

"I think you said, 'See you in court.'"

"That's pretty close. I said, "I've seen your legal work. That's not much of a threat.'"

"So, except for the ex-employee, everyone is happy. Good job."

"I'm not so sure everyone sees it that way. Oh. Did I mention he's Black?"

"Aha! That's why the White bosses didn't kick him out. They were afraid they would be labeled as racists."

"Right. But they put up with him for years. You think I'm *not* being called a racist over this?"

"I don't know."

"I'm only guessing. No one has said anything to me about it, yet."

---

"Did you notice that your fountain is bubbling over with soap suds?"

"Yeah. Kids do that from time to time. Not just this fountain."

"At least the FTC wasn't singled out."

"My lawyers working on the detergent rule think it is aimed at them, by the manufacturers. One even called it a 'gangster threat.'"

"I guess they think they are being menaced with a good scrubbing for their clothes."

"Let me tell you about the most pleasant file review I've ever had."

"Who reviewed your files?"

"No one reviews my files. I go through the written work of my lawyers."

"I'll bet they love that."

"They hate it. Who wouldn't?"

"But today was different?"

"Absolutely. Remember that lawyer I fired?"

"Yeah."

"At the end of that same review period I warned another one he was going to be fired if he didn't spend more time on FTC work."

"What was his excuse?"

"He is a general in the Army Reserve and he was also coordinating the United Way Campaign."

"At least those are both government gigs."

"But not the one the FTC is paying him to do."

"So, he took your notice seriously?"

"He did indeed. His work is all up to date. And he even thanked me for giving him a second chance."

---

"Put your seat belt on, Barbara. How was your Monday?"

"I don't know."

"What happened?"

"Last week several women complained about a division chief who has been giving them 'good morning' and 'good evening' kisses for a long time."

"Hmm."

"You know Linda, the other female Assistant Director."

"Of course. I know her husband Bob, the rocket scientist, and their little girl Brie, too."

"Okay. Okay. Let me tell you about this. Linda and I were tasked with investigating. We checked to see if the Commission had ever had a sexual harassment complaint before."

"Good idea."

"They did indeed have a very similar situation. A division chief who liked to pat women's butts in passing."

"What did the Director do about that?"

"Nothing. Well, next to nothing. The man was cautioned. He promised to keep his hands off female fannies and life went on unabated."

"So, what are you and Linda going to do?"

"We're done."

"Oh."

"First, we interviewed the women. Then we sat down with their boss on Friday. He was shocked. He thought they liked being treated like beloved family members."

"Amazing."

"This morning, he called his entire division together and apologized to the women. He said a man as insensitive to the feelings of others as he has been should not be in charge. And he resigned."

"What!"

"That's right. He submitted his resignation and left. The rumor mill says that Linda and I got the Commission to fire him, but we haven't even submitted our report yet."

"So, what's the blowback going to be?"

"We don't know. We do know that he has been one of the most productive division chiefs. Very popular. Even the women who complained are not happy we caused him to resign."

"Did you suggest he quit?"

"Absolutely not.

One fall day, Barbara hopped in the car with good news. "I know you have lots of leave on the books. I hope you can take these twenty days off." She handed me a note.

"I can put in a request. Where are we going?"

"We have an all-expenses-paid trip to Aspen, Colorado."

"I'll have to get permission to accept that. Who's paying?"

"The Aspen Institute."

"What kind of institute is that?"

"It's a place where corporate executives have been studying the humanities for the past thirty years."

"The humanities?"

She looked at a piece of paper. "They 'read the works of classic and modern writers to better understand the human challenges facing organizations and the communities they serve.'"

"Read? I'll have to read a ton of stuff?"

"I'll read the material and tell you about it. If the FBI will let you go, you'll be accompanying me as my spouse, not as a participant."

"What does the spouse job entail?"

"I'm guessing fashion shows, shopping trips, maybe a little yoga, or classes on floral arrangements." She giggled.

"So, you will be with the men, and I will be with the women?"

"We'll be together in the evenings. And we may get to meet some serious thinkers." She referred to the document, again. "They have had presentations by Albert Schweitzer, Thornton Wilder, Arthur Rubinstein, Ernest Hemingway, Jose Ortega y Gasset …"

"My uncle!"

"You're kidding."

"I didn't start it, but there was a rumor at the University of Puerto Rico when I was a student there that I was the nephew of Jose Ortega y Gasset, because of our similar last names."

"And you never corrected it?"

"No one ever asked me directly."

---

Before I tell you about our adventures with the Aspen Institute, let me cap off my recall of the Federal Trade Commission with a heartwarming story.

Decades after Barbara left, she got an invitation to attend the retirement of a man who held her old position.

"Want to go?" she asked me.

"Do you know this guy?"

"I hired him. But I haven't spoken to him for over thirty years."

"Maybe your invite is just a formality. And they don't expect you to actually show up."

"Not likely. He wrote a personal note on it. He really wants me to come."

"I'd like to see your old office. So, yes. I want to go."

The more things change, the more they stay the same. Barbara's office had different wallpaper, and all the lawyers were strangers, but the atmosphere felt just as it did when she was there.

After being praised by several speakers, the honoree took the podium.

"First, I would like to introduce the woman who is responsible for my long career here. Her name is Barbara Rowan and she's sitting right back there."

Barbara smiled, but I knew she didn't like the spotlight.

He went on. "Barbara, do you recall what you said when you first interviewed me?"

Barbara laughed and nodded.

He told the crowd, "She said, 'Get out of my office … and come back next year.'"

Then he answered our puzzled looks.

"You see, I had graduated first in my law school class, and I was sincerely interested in the mission of the FTC. However, I had been invited to crew on a sailboat that was going to circumnavigate the earth, so I was torn between accepting an appointment here, or sailing around the world."

The crowd murmured.

"After telling me to get out of her office, Barbara wisely pointed out that if I started working here, I would no doubt get married, have children, and a mortgage, etc. And I would never have the opportunity to take that carefree adventure trip, again."

Ooos and Aaas stirred the air.

"'Come back next year and I will hire you,' she said.

'But I will start a year behind my classmates.'

'Yes, but you shall have seen the world. That experience will give you an enormous advantage over those who have only seen the inside of law books.'

I am so glad you could come today, Barbara, so I can thank you publicly for changing my entire life for the better."

# CHAPTER TWENTY
## *The Aspen Institute*

"Are you going to the Aspen Institute?" asked a chipper young woman as we got on the bus at the Aspen Airport.

"Yes, we are," said Barbara.

"Good. We may be in the same seminar. My name is Margi."

I would have guessed her to be in her late teens. I was only about ten years off. She owned a public relations company in New York City. A grandmother now, Margi still looks younger than her years. She is the best listener that Barbara and I ever knew.

At the institute that evening we met the rest of our class.

CEOs from a major oil company, a national insurance company, a well-known telephone company, and two world class manufacturing firms, as well as a partner in a Wall Street brokerage firm, a business consultant, Margi, and a corporate public relations expert, represented private industry.

Barbara and a White House attorney were there as federal regulators. He was working on President Carter's efforts to require automakers to build cars which belched out less $CO_2$.

The state regulator among us was a Public Utilities Commissioner from Idaho, who had been a longtime newspaperman, and state lawmaker.

An International Ladies Garment Workers Union executive spoke for labor. He introduced himself as a buttonhole maker but was the solitary one of us who could quote the Federalist Papers.

Only the two public relations people were single. We spouses of the other participants were each required to introduce ourselves to the group.

The corporate wives were all active in social and charitable causes.

The wife of the White House lawyer said, "My only goal in life is to keep Peter happy." Unaware of her wry sense of humor, and her extensive business background as a corporate executive, many present thought she was serious.

I was the first FBI employee to attend the Aspen Institute. I couldn't tell how the others felt about that.

The next morning, we learned the system. Each participant had a name plate they could stand on end if they had something to say. If the moderator called on someone else first, and they changed their mind, they could put their nameplate down.

Spouses witnessed the discussions silently from the audience. Well, not entirely silently. To my surprise nearly all the well-quaffed corporate wives brought their knitting. That's right, knitting.

At one point Barbara put up her name plate, was called on, and said, "Gentlemen, I believe some of your wives would like to say something."

"Why would you think so, Barbara?"

"Can't you hear those knitting needles? When your remarks raise their blood pressure, the needles click faster and faster."

That led to a discussion, which resulted in a decision to allow the spouses to participate.

Like those knitting needles, opinions clicked together and created something valuable.

For example, a CEO of a manufacturing company complained about the Occupational Safety and Health Administration. "Of course, we want to keep our employees safe, but those OSHA people are nit-picking us to death."

Our union man said, "Workplace safety standards came about due to the Triangle Shirtwaist Factory fire in New York City in 1911. It killed 146 garment workers because they were locked inside during their shifts. We can't rely on management to keep us safe."

"Well, there you have it," a wife said, "both sides of the argument: management and labor."

"Our criminal court system is designed to improve future behavior by punishing wrongdoers," said Barbara. "However, it cuts both ways. The defense tries the government's case while the prosecution tries the defendant. And that's a good thing."

She let that soak in for a couple of seconds.

"The owners of the Triangle Shirtwaist Factory were charged with Manslaughter, but the defense attorney impeached a key witness, one of the teen-agers who was trapped in the building, by doing something we would never get away with today. On cross examination, he simply asked her to repeat her heart-wrenching story. Everyone was stunned. The judge asked, 'You want the jury to hear all that again?' 'Yes, your honor.'"

Barbara's timing was perfect. She waited till several name plates turned up before she continued.

"After the young woman went through her long painful testimony a second time, the judge broke for lunch. When they came back, the defense continued the cross by asking the young woman to refresh the jury's recollection by telling her tale a third time. She did so. Word for word.

"It dawned on everyone that her story was memorized.

"The defense attorney suggested that all the wit-nesses were merely spouting testimony concocted by the prosecution.

"The owners of the factory were acquitted."

Our retired insurance company CEO added to our Triangle fire knowledge. "Barbara told you about the criminal case, but there was a civil case as well. The owners lost that one and had to pay $75 to each of the families of the deceased. Dollars were worth ten times as much back then."

"Seven hundred and fifty dollars for a human life," said our union man. "You would have to pay more than that if you ran into someone's horse."

I had to put in my two cents worth. "There is at least one other side to this story. The cops from the Mercer Street Station had responded to a strike at the shirtwaist factory the year before. They had driven the women away with their night sticks.

"On the day of the fire, they watched some of the teenagers they had poked with their batons leaping from tenth floor windows screaming with their clothes and hair on fire and plummeting to the pavement. The policemen heard the sickening thuds that silenced those young women forever."

"You know one of those cops?" the business consultant asked.

"No. I spent a night on surveillance with an NYPD detective whose grandfather was one of those hapless policemen. He said his granddad never got over watching those immigrant teenagers die a horrible death."

Our buttonhole maker said, "I wrote a book about the Triangle fire. While researching it, I met a mounted cop who rode his horse right into the burning building and up the stairs. At each level the horse kicked the doors open so people could escape, but some of the stairs had been burned away so the horse couldn't reach the top floors."

Our deliberations continued outside the conference room. We took our meals together, skied together, went shopping and hit the hot tub and saunas together. Well, the hot tub was coed, but only a few of us got in. And the saunas were gender specific.

The more we shared our experiences and opinions, the more we liked one another. By the end of our seminar, we did something unprecedented. We scheduled a reunion.

Like Aspen, we would have material to read beforehand about a relevant topic, and we would invite a significant guest speaker. None of us had another 20 days to spare, but we could handle a four-day weekend.

Our first reunion was in New York City. Everyone's attitude toward Margi changed. Her public relations firm was not a little hobby shop. She had lots of employees and she leased a considerable amount of expensive mid-town office space.

That meeting went so well, we did it again, and again, for over 25 years.

We took turns hosting the annual get-togethers. Barbara and I hosted one in Alexandria, Virginia. Other Aspen weekends were held in Los Angeles; Houston; Kansas City; Montreal; Charleston; Boise; Jackson Hole; San Antonio; Washington, D.C.; Newport, Rhode Island; etc.

Such bonding was so unusual that The Aspen Institute sometimes sent representatives to monitor our meetings. They hoped to find out what kept us coming together annually.

Both our PR people got married and we welcomed their spouses. One couple got divorced but both remained part of our extended family. We took in the co-founder of the Public Citizen Litigation Group, an alumnus of the Aspen Institute, and his wife.

Of course, over time we have lost one member after another, because nobody lives forever.

# CHAPTER TWENTY-ONE
## *Rowan Associates*

"I'm not your friend. I'm your lawyer. I represent your rights. Your rights have been offended. Don't ever think we're pals."

I heard Barbara's voice as I climbed the stairs to her new law office in Olde Towne Alexandria. I expected to see a gangster client, but no, the woman coming out of her office was gorgeous, a former finalist in the Miss America Contest.

"What did she do to deserve a scolding?" I asked, after the other beautiful Black woman was gone.

"She invited me to a church picnic."

At the trial, I learned that the preacher's pretty wife was coming home from the gym one Friday evening clad only in a leotard and shoes when two White police officers mistook her for a fugitive they were seeking. They wouldn't let her enter her house to get her ID and they ignored the police officer who lived next door. He assured them she was not their target.

The arresting officers handcuffed the woman and dragged her into their police car by her hair. Booked into the county jail she had to await further action until Monday morning. Fortunately, on Sunday a jailer who knew the fugitive from prior incarcerations released the upstanding citizen.

Of course, the beauty queen looked nothing like the fugitive, other than being a Black female of approximately the same age.

Barbara had returned to private practice because her mother's health was failing. She could do a lot of her legal work at home while watching over Clara.

---

"If you can take the time off, Harry, I've found us another all-expenses-paid vacation. I've got someone to stay with mom."

"A vacation where?"

"Miami Beach."

"My old stomping grounds. Who's picking up the tab?"

"The folks who sell franchises."

By way of explanation, I will use McDonald's as an example, although I don't recall them being represented at the conference. A brand name retailer can sell franchises to folks who want to own one of their restaurants, shops, garages, etc. In addition to the purchase price, the franchisees pay fees for using the name and technology as well as charges for national advertising.

"Why would they want us there?" I asked.

"The FTC issued rules for franchising and, since I was involved in that, the Commission has asked me if I would help explain those rules to the industry."

In Miami Beach, I watched Barbara do her presentation.

"I know this may seem complicated, so I have set aside the remainder of my time for questions. Anyone have a question?"

Did they ever! The Q&A went on for hours. And which FTC rules were they concerned about? None that I recall. What they wanted to know was how could they tell when a franchisee was cheating them.

In those days, the payments were a percentage of sales. But who reported the sales? The franchisees.

I was proud of my spouse. She suggested numerous investigative techniques tailored to the different businesses. And she explained the legal pitfalls of some of their ideas.

For example, several company executives wanted to hire private investigators to go to work for their franchisees and secretly monitor their activities.

"Absolutely not," said Barbara. "An employee has a legal duty to be loyal to their employer. Once your investigator goes on their payroll, you can't pay them to betray that trust."

Later, Barbara told me that several conferees had tried to retain her.

"Why not?" I asked.

"That's not the kind of law I want to practice. But I'll tell you what I'm thinking about. I could do investigative consulting."

"Many former FBI agents conduct private investigations," I said. "So, there is a nationwide network of reliable guys you could hire to monitor franchisees."

And thus, Rowan Associates was born.

---

"Sorry I'm late, sweetheart."

"No. Tis I who fixed dinner too early," she joked.

"Seriously. You look stressed."

"I'm an FBI agent's wife. We know you guys could be putting yourselves in danger anytime you are out of our sight."

"We have female agents now too, you know."

"No doubt their husbands fret about them."

"You seem more anxious than usual."

"I am. I'm scared to death that I'm going to make a fool of myself."

"How?"

"I told the franchise folks I'm available for consulting."

"Yes, we discussed that."

"And a franchiser from Texas wants me to come down and solve his problems."

"So?"

"It's gonna involve numbers, Harry. I don't do numbers."

"Right. What are you going to tell him?"

"I demanded a huge retainer, hoping he would find someone else. But he said, 'no problem.'"

"Why don't you take Marvin with you?"

"Oh, my darling! You are a genius! I was only thinking about hiring investigators."

"Marv is an investigator."

"Yeah, but he is also a fabulous forensic accountant."

By way of background, I can tell you that I had met Marvin a decade earlier, in New York City. I was working stolen securities cases. A confidential source said a crook had shown him a briefcase full of stolen stock certificates and had placed it in the trunk of a red Cadillac convertible. The informant got the tag number.

I traced it to an address in Manhattan and found the car parked on the street. While I was trying to figure out how I could get a search warrant without burning my source, a tow truck rolled up. The driver got out and hooked up the Cadillac.

The bad guy rushed out and said, "Hey! That's my car."

The tow truck driver said, "Not anymore. I'm with the Internal Revenue Service and I've seized it, for non-payment of federal income taxes."

The subject said, "My briefcase is in the trunk. Can I get it out?"

"What's in it?"

"Stock certificates."

"I'm seizing them too."

At this point, the tough guy attacked the IRS man, so I arrested him for Assaulting a Federal Officer.

Marvin was the federal officer. We became fast friends. After we both married, our wives were pals as well. We even got our Yorkshire terriers at the same place.

Coincidentally, the Internal Revenue Service loaned Marv to the House of Representatives to work on the Koreagate investigation at the same time Barbara and I worked there. Marv lived in our house while his new Virginia home was being built.

---

"How was your flight?" I asked Barbara when I picked her up at the airport.

"Boring. Not like the meeting in Texas."

"Tell me about it."

"When Marv and I were shown into the big boss's office, he was writing the retainer check. He slid it across the desk. I slid it right back to him and said, 'I'm not taking your money till you tell me what the problem is.'

"He said, 'I've got a gut feeling my franchisees are underreporting.' He pushed the check back toward me.

"I said, 'I've got a piece of evidence to support your feeling. What do you have?' I slipped the check over to him, again.

"He shoved the check back to my side of the desktop. 'I told you. A gut feeling. What evidence could you possibly have?'

"I returned the check and said, 'In you waiting room I saw three newsletters.'

"'Yeah. They come out every month.'

"'And on the front page there is an article about the most productive location. Right?'

"'Right.'

"'The most productive franchisee last month had only been open for three months. The other two had merely been in business for four months.'

"'So?'

"'So, how come all your well-established franchisees are less profitable than the new ones?'

"A light bulb came on over his head. 'You mean after a few months they figure out I can't really tell how much they sell?'

"Marv started laughing. 'You two are gonna wear that check out. Surely, sir, you must have…' And he reeled off a list of records that a normal business would generate.

"The guy looked like he was going to cry. 'No. I don't have any of that. I do business on a handshake.'

"So, I said, 'Since you paid for first-class airfare, and our return flight isn't for three hours, I'll read a copy of your franchise agreements, while Marv explains how you can put your network on a business basis. If you can get that done, I will reconsider taking you on as a client."

I don't know if she ever did. But she took on other franchise firms.

Each time a client had to close a franchisee for underreporting, the income from all the other locations in their network doubled for a month or two.

Policing misbehavior is a never-ending task, but well worth the cost.

Due to attorney/client privilege, Barbara did not tell me who her clients were, but I could see she was getting busier and busier.

She did mention that law firms who represented franchisers hired her for other matters after they had seen her work.

And some of her former colleagues from the U.S. Attorney's Office in New York hired her to manage their investigative needs.

Rowan Associates also consulted with some of our Aspen Institute conferees whose huge corporations suffered their share of financial frauds.

Clara passed away in 1982, just before Christmas.

Barbara and I found it difficult to stay in the house that she was so much a part of, so we, and our two remaining Yorkshire terriers, moved to a condominium in Alexandria, Virginia.

That shortened our commutes by a couple hours each day. We certainly needed all the time we could get. Barbara was so busy she was referring clients to other investigative firms she could trust to do honest inquires. I was supervising government corruption squads in the FBI Washington Field Office.

Then a perfect storm brought us together for almost all our waking hours.

In those days, the FBI was the only organization I knew of where everyone was struggling to stay at the bottom. *Special Agent* was the best job in the Bureau.

Management techniques were prescribed by Congress and the courts, so they were cumbersome.

As a field supervisor I got to see FBI agents every day, support their investigations as best I could, and encourage their efforts.

On major cases I was out there with them directing their work, but otherwise I was expected to be at my desk in the field office. My windows overlooked the Anacostia River and the forest surrounding it.

The next step up the hierarchy would be a desk in a windowless office at FBI Headquarters where I would be reading documents all day (communications written by Special Agents) and finding something to criticize, perhaps the punctuation, to show I had done my job.

For a dyslexic like me that would have been the tenth circle of hell.

In fact, most field supervisors did not want to go to headquarters. The Director was having difficulty staffing positions there. So, he made advancement mandatory.

I was promoted and I couldn't get out of it. Although I was too young to retire, I had spent twenty years in the FBI so, coupled with my Marine Corps time, I could collect a federal retirement later.

But most of all, Barbara needed me. Working with her sounded heavenly to me. And that proved to be the case.

"I don't know if we can stand each other if we are together twenty-four hours a day," said Barbara.

"I don't either, but I hope so. If we start to drive one another crazy, I'll get a job somewhere else. Okay?"

"We could take separate vacations," she said.

"That doesn't sound like any fun."

"I would understand if you had an affair."

"That doesn't sound like any fun, either. I can't believe you would forgive me."

"I wouldn't forgive you, Harry."

"You'd divorce me."

"No. I don't believe in divorce. But I do believe in homicide."

As it happened, we never needed time apart. We couldn't do our office work in the same room—we interrupted one another when we tried. But in separate offices, with only a wall between us, we were close enough to maintain contact and to defer to one another's strong points.

"I manage words and Harry does the numbers," Barbara often told people. She did the bulk of the reading and wrote all the legal papers. I handled financial records, which are essential evidence in business fraud cases.

We both conducted interviews, often together, and each of us managed independent contractors, or "associates," as we called them.

Working together was always delightful. We used the same system we had agreed to twelve years earlier on route to Bedford–Stuyvesant in the middle of the night. Whenever we interviewed anyone, particularly potential clients, whichever spouse they spoke to carried on the conversation.

Since Barbara was a successful trial lawyer, attorneys often addressed her. Most of the male non-lawyers directed their comments to me. Surprisingly, females were a toss-up.

The first important business lesson I learned from Barbara was, "The clients we don't take are more important than the ones we do."

That didn't make sense at first.

She explained, "When someone wants us to investigate their lawyers who represented them when they sued their accountants, you know they are going to blame us next, if we let them retain us. Just say 'no.'"

Potential clients were often surprised when we turned them away. What kind of business doesn't want your business? Our scrupulous little boutique, that's who.

For example, a wealthy guy shot a bear from his plane in Alaska, in violation of the law. A state trooper saw him do it and arrested him when he landed. The shooter wanted us to dig up some dirt on the arresting officer with which he could blackmail the lawman to get him to change his eye-witness testimony.

Barbara said, "You didn't get into this trouble by being a good citizen. And now you want to double down and go after an honest cop? You should find the best lawyer in Alaska to negotiate a good plea deal for you. We certainly won't help you."

Since clients of Rowan Associates signed engagement agreements with Barbara Ann Rowan,

Attorney at Law, I cannot disclose their identities or cases, due to lawyer/client privilege. However, I can describe them generically.

During the thirty-five years we worked together, we conducted over 1,800 investigations for:

Agricultural firms

Airlines

Airports

Art galleries

Banks

Bar Associations

Bestselling non-fiction authors

Boat owners

Business publications

Casinos

Computer distributors

Churches

City governments

Department store chains

Families of missing persons

Film makers

Franchisers

Hospitals

Hotels

International package delivery firms

International trading companies

Insurance companies

Investment firms

Investors

Labor unions

Law firms

Nursing homes

Other investigative firms

Pharmaceutical companies

Private schools

Public relations firms

Publishers

Real Estate firms

Restaurants

Telephone companies

Theatre owners

Tractor manufacturers

Travel agencies

TV networks

Universities

Wall Street brokerage firms

Note: All the above descriptions are plural. That often came about because the CEO or Chief Counsel at one firm would be hired by another in the same industry and discover a financial fraud problem similar to one we had solved at their last place of employment.

We were only hired by one:

Bottling company

Candy manufacturer

International music production company

In addition, a few client organizations are unique. I can't describe them without divulging their identities.

We didn't invent the gig economy, in fact we called it "cottage industry," but we hired independent contractors on a case-by-case basis at a time when most companies wanted to keep their workers where they could watch them.

Some of our investigations involved undercover operations. Barbara refused to participate in those personally. She thought it unethical for an attorney to misrepresent her identity and purpose. She certainly didn't mind if I and other associates penetrated criminal conspiracies in covert roles, so long as we obeyed the laws.

How much work did each case require? That varied enormously. Some involved only a few phone calls. Others were colossal projects.

On several occasions, we had over a hundred subcontractors working on many parts of the same inquiry simultaneously.

We investigated a matter that resulted in the largest civil settlement in the history of the United States. And the largest criminal fine ever levied in the USA. It held the same two distinctions in the European Union.

In addition, we provided training to:

City, county, state, and federal law enforcement agencies

Corporate executives

State societies of Certified Public Accountants

Trial Lawyers Associations

U.S. intelligence officers from several agencies

Long before Google was devised, the World Wide Web had databases which could be tasked for various types of information by those who were willing to pay for access and knew the complex protocols used to query each archive.

For example, there was a database of all official records of U.S. state legislatures.

We contacted the major players in the database business, and they were very cooperative. They introduced us to some of their best computer programmers who were no longer full-time employees—women on maternity leave, for example.

With one additional partner, we set up a computer research subsidiary. On behalf of our clients, our battery of home bodies could collect data at their convenience, perhaps when the kids were asleep.

Using the above example of legislature databases, we routinely checked to see if a certain snack food was mentioned by lawmakers anywhere in the USA. If so, our client, that product's manufacturers' association, sent lawyers and lobbyists to try to prevent the passage of laws affecting sales of their eatables.

When Google became available, we sold our cyber research company.

One of the buyers asked, "What happens when one of your contractors slips and falls in the kitchen. Is that a work-related injury?"

I said, "I don't know. It's never happened. But if it did, it would cost less than buying a building."

In fact, the new owners did obtain a building and required the researchers to work there. Of course, that change drove up costs and reduced productivity, but the last time I checked they were still in business.

We also founded a publishing company to print and distribute three editions of: *Handbook on State Laws Regarding Secretly Recording Your Own Conversations, by Barbara Ann Rowan, Attorney at Law.*

Self-publishing in those days required us to print a supply of hard copies, rent warehouse space to store them, and engage a shipper to send them out to fulfill orders.

# CHAPTER TWENTY-TWO
# *The President's Commission on Organized Crime*

"I'm sorry you chose to resign, Harry."

I looked up and discovered I was being address by the FBI Director.

We were sitting in folding chairs in the White House Rose Garden. He was on the front row with his Organized Crime Section Chief. I was at the back. Between us sat the families of folks who were there to be sworn in as Organized Crime Commissioners. The appointees were standing near the podium. Barbara was one of them.

"I'm relieved to learn you got my resignation letter," I said. "I gave you thirty days' notice, so I left after thirty days, but I didn't know for sure till today that I was no longer on the rolls."

He laughed.

That was the only bright spot during that dismal wait for the President to appear. It was one of those miserably hot, humid Washington summer days and everyone there was wearing substantial clothing for the big event.

Periodically, someone would come out of the White House to assure us that President Reagan was still tied up with an urgent matter of national importance. But he would be with us shortly.

After broiling for an eternity, I was afraid I was going to pass out. Later, I feared I might not. I'm sure the rest of the soggy mass felt the same way.

Suddenly, President Reagan bounded out of the building. He was cheerful and delightful. His rosy cheeks were made up and his eyes twinkled.

He started with a laugh line: "Let me get you folks sworn in, so I can get back to my airconditioned office." We all laughed.

Solemnly, he swore in the commissioners as a group and then sat down to sign their individual commissions. As he called out their names, each stepped up to accept their document, a handshake, and a jolly congratulation, as well as the pen with which the President had signed them into their commissionership.

Barbara gave her pen to one of the kids in the audience after the head of state left.

As his next inauguration approached, we received an engraved invitation from President Ronald Reagan himself. It came with a cover letter advising that we were not authorized to enter any of the inaugural events, but the invitation was "suitable for framing."

Immediately after we left the Rose Garden, in our airconditioned car, we rushed to cover a lead at a client's construction site. Despite our best business clothing, including Barbara's highest heels, no one noticed us because we put on hard hats and carried clipboards.

We split up to cover the area quicker. Barbara shouted to me. "Don't forget to rinky-dink the rack-a-frack." Making noise is a technique intended to cause others to ignore you. If you were sneaking around, you wouldn't be shouting right?

Later, Barbara would explain that in her over-heated condition she couldn't think of any construction terms. But it didn't matter because no one was close enough to wonder about the gibberish. Workers only heard some woman shouting orders.

"Don't forget to rinky-dink the rack-a-frack," became our way of telling one another that we were confused.

The day after being wilted in the Rose Garden, the female spouses and I were treated to a tour of FBI Headquarters while the new commissioners had their first meeting.

The last stop on the tour was the firing range where an FBI agent demonstrated the weapons FBI agents must learn to shoot proficiently.

As it happened, the agent who had that duty was an old friend. He said, "Hey, Harry. You wanna shoot the tommy gun for them?"

"Nah. You go ahead."

If any of the women had not heard the FBI Director's comments earlier, they all now knew I had some connection with the Bureau.

"What the hell happened, honey?" I asked Barbara as she trudged to the car. "You look shell shocked."

"I couldn't think of anything funny to say."

"About what?"

"You know Strom Thurmond."

"Yeah. He helped us out with the Abscam."

Abscam was an FBI undercover operation which netted several corrupt congressmen. I supervised the trial phase and Senator Strom Thurmond's cooperation assisted our successful prosecutive efforts.

Barbara said, "You no doubt noticed that he was sworn in as a commissioner yesterday."

"I didn't get to speak to him, but I saw him there."

"He was late to our first meeting, so everyone else was seated when he arrived. All the commissioners rose and greeted him as he walked the length of the room toward me. He merely smiled at them individually, but he grabbed my face with both hands and kissed me right on my mouth!"

"What!"

"I pushed him away and wiped off his kiss. Everyone thought it was funny."

"I can't imagine you being speechless."

"No. I wasn't speechless. I said, 'Don't you ever do that again!' But that only got a second laugh. At my expense."

"Strom's in his 80s. He must be getting senile. I could have a word with him."

"Don't you dare! I'll take care of the old racist."

Barbara was right to call Strom a racist. He ran for President in 1948 as a Dixiecrat, promising to maintain racial segregation in America. He performed the longest single-person filibuster in U.S. history in opposition to a 1957 Civil Rights Act. And he joined the Republican Party when President Lyndon Johnson, a Democrat, signed the Civil Rights Act of 1964 into law.

---

"Did you get another open mouth kiss from Strom today?" I asked my lovely wife after the second meeting of the Organized Crime Commission.

"God knows he tried. I put my hand up, so he only kissed the heel of my hand."

"So, you weren't dumbstruck?"

"Oh, no. He was the butt of the joke this time."

"Who would ever guess that federal organized crime commissioners were playing kindergarten games?"

"It's an unpaid job, so we might as well have fun while we are looking into the dark side of the American economy."

"Why is Strom trying to embarrass you?"

"He's not. I think he really likes me. He supported every comment I made at this meeting."

I said, "He reminds me of that guy at the Federal Trade Commission who thought all the women in his office enjoyed a kiss from him."

---

"What a circus," Barbara said when I picked her up after she presented the commission's final recommendations to a congressional committee.

"What happened?"

"We made over 200 proposals for new federal laws. The President supports them all. But the entire hearing only focused on one."

"Which was?"

"We suggested that commercial pilots, train engineers, and truck drivers be given random drug tests."

"Were there junkies on the congressional committee?"

"No. Just a showboat. Congressman Ackerman. He also chairs the Post Office and Civil Service subcommittee on human resources."

"So?"

"Some postal employees drive big trucks."

"And he doesn't mind if they're stoned?"

"Apparently not. He asked Rod to pee in a cup before the hearing got started."

Rod was the deputy executive director of the organized crime commission. He had accompanied Barbara to the hearing.

"Was the wiseass willing to hold the cup."

"We should have asked him to. He gave the press the impression that we wanted all federal employees to provide random urine samples under the direct observation of a manager. So, he wanted Rod to take a congressional staffer to the men's room with him to watch him fill the cup."

"What happened?"

"I said for the record, 'these hearings are supposed to be serious matters, not humorous matters' and the request was 'inappropriate.'"

"Right."

"And I told Rod to be prepared to storm out, since we were not under subpoena."

"Go on."

"Ackerman insisted that it *was* a serious matter and demanded Rod's compliance.

"Rod said we had been given no prior notice that a drug test would be required, and he would explain our drug-testing proposal in his testimony.

"Ackerman said that federal employees would be given no notice so Rod should give a sample before he was allowed to testify.

"I said Rod would absolutely not be providing any urine. We stood up to leave, but the congressman declared that he had proven his point and the hearing went on."

I told my bride, "I'll bet the pissing match is the only thing the press will report."

I was right about that.

---

"Hey, Harry, do you remember Justin Dintino from the Organized Crime Commission?"

"I do remember him, Barbara. He was a New Jersey state trooper. Started off as a motorcycle trooper."

"Right. Now Justin has been promoted. He's going to be the Superintendent of the New Jersey State Police."

"Good choice. He's a straight arrow."

"After his swearing in, there's going to be a dinner for him. He's asked us to come."

"Great!"

When we got there, we selected a table at the back of the room.

"So how do you know Colonel Dintino?" asked a petite White woman seated next to Barbara.

"I don't answer questions from strangers," said Barbara.

"I'm a reporter," said the woman.

"I particularly don't like being interviewed by reporters."

"My boyfriend here is a captain in the state police. Think you can get home without a ticket?"

The boyfriend nodded.

After truckloads of praise were dumped on the honoree, he finally got to speak.

"First of all, I'd like to thank my dear friend Barbara Rowan for driving all the way up here from Washington, D.C. We served together on the Organized Crime Commission. It's so good to have you here, Barbara."

My wife smiled through a round of applause. Then she turned to the reporter. "You still think I can't get home without a ticket?"

Justin acknowledged other folks as well before he told the troopers just what he expected of them. "It is important that we enforce the laws, but just as important that we obey the laws."

He pointed out the mounting number of confirmed complaints by motorists, and he detailed a few of the more egregious behaviors which seemed to have become standard procedure for some in his department.

Those corrupt practices would no longer be tolerated, much less defended.

We got home without a ticket and Justin did a housecleaning in New Jersey.

---

"Sit down, Harry. I want to read this to you."

"What happened?"

"Strom Thurmond died."

"That's no surprise. He was over a hundred years old."

This conversation occurred about twenty years after the President's Commission on Organized Crime.

"That's not the interesting part. Turns out he had a Black daughter."

"When?"

"When he was twenty-two. His White family apparently knew this all along. They pointed out that he was single at the time he 'had a romance with her mother, a maid in the Thurmond home.'"

"How old was the maid?"

"Fifteen or sixteen."

"I wonder where he took her to dinner, and which movies they went to see together."

"She couldn't have gone into a restaurant or movie theatre in South Carolina in 1925!"

"I was being sarcastic, Barbara. 'Had a romance' is such a southern way to say he raped the Black maid."

Several folks from the organized crime commission called Barbara to say they now understood why Senator Thurmond liked her so much. She reminded him of his Black daughter.

I heard her ask them: "Have you seen her picture? She looks nothing like me, and she's dozen years older than I am."

After one of those conversations, I suggested, "Perhaps you reminded him of his daughter's mother. I don't think her picture has been published."

"You don't understand, Harry. White supremacists think Black people are less evolved and more animalistic, hence, sexier."

"I think you're sexier."

"You would."

## CHAPTER TWENTY-THREE
# *Twentieth Century Travel*

"Why did you buy these file folders?" I asked Barbara early in our marriage. "Doesn't the U.S. Attorney's Office supply stuff like that?"

"These are for my own private files."

"You have private files?

"Not yet, but I'm going to."

"What for?"

"Places we are going to travel to."

"Looks like we are going to a lot of places."

"That's my plan."

"Great! What goes in the files?"

"Notes about things I learn from friends, and books, or hear on the radio. And I plan to clip travel articles out of newspapers and magazines."

"So will you have files on cities or countries?"

"Mainly cities. So, when we get to go to Paris or Rome, we can read up on what we ought to see there."

"You've been to Paris and Rome."

"You haven't," she said.

"Sounds like a lot of reading."

"It's a long flight."

"I've never been to Europe, but you haven't seen much of the United States."

"Right. I'll start files on cities here, as well. I want to see all the state capitol buildings. And national parks, too."

Starting in those pre-Wikipedia days, Barbara's travel dossiers served us well for over five hundred and eighty months, prepping us for vacations and business trips.

---

"Cripes! That movie was scary," said Barbara as we walked back toward the sloop we had rented.

"The fact that we were watching it in the very room where the shark hunter explained to the city fathers what the man-eating shark would do if they didn't hire him made it special."

Edgartown, Massachusetts, didn't have a theatre, so they had shown the movie *Jaws* in their Townhall, since it was filmed there.

"No, Harry. It was the music. I'll be hearing that in my dreams, knowing we will be sailing out into that shark's habitat tomorrow morning."

"I'm more worried about the weather. Our thirty-six-foot Pearson is bigger than what we usually sail, but the Atlantic is far larger than the Chesapeake Bay. We might encounter higher waves than we have sailed in before."

Barbara suffered her nightmares, and I got my bad weather.

The waves got bigger and bigger as we departed the harbor. We were towing a thirteen-foot Boston Waler in case we sunk the Pearson. A Boston Waler has a foam filled hull so it cannot sink.

Once out of sight of land, plowing into fifteen-foot whitecaps soon had us bobbing like a fishing cork in the rain.

Barbara was at the helm.

"Let's come about for Edgartown, Barbara. This is no fun."

"I was hoping you would say that."

With a following sea our situation calmed a bit.

"Harry, everything in the cabin has been tossed around."

"I'll secure the gear."

After I stowed and lashed down the sail bags, I picked up our lunch basket, took out a sandwich and bit into it.

Looking up I could see Barbara silhouetted against the angry sky.

"We are about to drown! And you're eating!"

"I don't want to die on an empty stomach."

Behind her head I saw the huge gray monster on the top of a wave diving right at her. It crashed on the thin metal rail behind her, then rose again.

The loud *BANG!* had caused her eyes to bulge. She didn't look back.

"The great white shark is eating the boat!"

I rushed up the ladder, tossed the sandwich in the ocean, and ran past Barbara, just as the Boston Waler surfed onto the rail a second time. ***BANG!***

With it close aboard I gathered the painter. (That's the tow rope to you land lubbers.) Snugged securely to the rail, our lifeboat stopped pounding on the stern.

We creeped back into the harbor at Edgartown having had our fill of the open ocean for the day.

———

Eleven years into our marriage, Rowan Associates gave us more control over our journeys. And many of them were work-related.

"Harry, I have clients from all over the place. Now that you are here with me, we can consult from anywhere. Is there a place you have lived that calls out to you? Please don't say somewhere in the South."

"I could be happy anywhere, so long as you're with me."

"Where would you like us to be?"

"I like southern California. It can get hot. Have you ever been there?"

"No. I have visited Mad Aunt Katherine in San Francisco."

Barbara's "Mad Aunt Katherine" was not a blood relative but had been a close friend of Barbara's parents. She was also not mad. A retired special educator, having taught challenged children for decades, Aunt Katherine spoke clearly and incredibly slowly.

Her pet peeve was hearing people call her hometown "Frisco." She pronounced it as four words: "San. Fran. Cis. Co." Her careful pronunciations made her seem slow witted. That gave her an advantage. She was smart, held advanced degrees, and was well traveled.

She had visited us in New York, where she lectured Bootsy about how much of her skin was showing, in her usual snail-paced style, as though she were scolding an uninformed urchin.

And she had once stayed with us in Virginia to keep Clara company during the day. I gave her a ride on the back of my motorcycle, and she got me to do that regularly.

While planning our future, I told Barbara, "I've never been to San Francisco. Is it as beautiful as they say?"

"Oh, yes. The fog comes in every morning and washes its face. It is warm enough for me to wear shorts all day and cool enough in the evenings to wear a fur coat."

"I've heard it is close enough to wine country to go to concerts in the vineyards."

"It is. Let's plan a business trip. If we get more clients out there, we will have a good reason to move."

We prepared a most inventive itinerary.

Armed with our national park pass, we packed up our camping gear, as well as some business clothes, and flew to San Diego.

There we met with a potential client, who didn't engage our services, but had given us an excuse to visit the oldest Spanish settlement on America's Pacific coast. I had been stationed there by the Marine Corps, so I showed Barbara around.

Then we changed clothes and drove our rental car inland to Joshua Tree National Park where we camped in the desert.

"What a storm, Harry! Are you sure it's just wind? Sounds like rain is pouring on the tent."

"That's sand. Hope it doesn't scour the paint off the rental car."

In the morning we discovered our pop tent had been blown about fifty yards away from the vehicle.

"Look at the scribbly trail we left in the sand," I said.

Barbara said, "I think it spells *A-r-n-o-l-d S-c-h-w-a-r-z-e-n-e-g-g-e-r.*"

After a day of touring Joshua Tree, we went back to the coast and checked into a hotel in Santa Monica where we scrubbed up before we visited another potential client. This one hired us many times during the next several years.

While in Santa Monica, we visited one of Barbara's aunts and her two daughters, and their big dog.

Then we played on the pier and swam in the ocean before we packed up and headed east to Death Valley National Park, the lowest terrain in the United States.

"No wonder they call it 'Death Valley,' Barbara. This is hotter than hell."

"I thought you were in the desert in the Marine Corps."

"I was. So, I can tell you that the surface all around us has got to be over 120 degrees Fahrenheit right now. If you were to get out and lie down, you would never get up."

"Those wild burros are laughing at us."

"They're amazing. In the middle of the day like this, they should be hiding in the shade."

"What shade? — Harry! The car's overheating!"

"Want to turn off the air conditioner? That might help."

"Can't you just pull over?"

"That would make it worse. We're almost there. Let's hope the engine doesn't seize before we get to a gas station or die from the heat."

At the Inn at Death Valley, we cooled off and met an interesting fellow who owned a manufacturing company and would become a client of our consulting firm.

Our next stop was Sequoia National Park. We went there to visit the General Grant Tree, a 3,000-year-old wonder. It's about 270 feet tall and over 100 feet around at its base. We brought it a gift.

"What language is he speaking?" I asked Barbara.

A man was talking to a video camera on a tripod with the Grant Tree behind him. He was the only human in sight.

"French," she said. "Parisian French."

We waited till he left before we sprinkled a few of Clara's ashes around the giant sequoia.

"May her beautiful spirit live on in this powerful tree," said Barbara.

Navigating Kings Canyon National Park was complicated by a visit from Queen Elizabeth II. We spent more time there than she did.

Then we drove to San Francisco where we visited one client and recruited another.

Aunt Katherine put us up in one of her Victorian houses.

We toured Presidio National Park in San-Fran-Cis-Co and then took off to the Modoc National Forest and Lava Beds National Monument in northeastern California.

On our way back to San Francisco for our return flight home, we stopped by Redding to meet with a CEO who hired us.

What an amazing blend of camping in the boondocks and meetings in executive offices.

"Why do you have different envelopes to store different receipts?" Barbara asked.

"Business and pleasure, mostly. For tax purposes. But I also separate charges applicable to different clients."

---

"The farther we go the longer we stay," became Barbara's slogan because she found long flights terribly confining.

Four days' work in New Zealand was followed by a month of touring there.

We divided the transoceanic fights into several shorter ones. For example, we flew from Virginia to Los Angeles and stayed there for a day or two, and then on to Honolulu for another break, and finally flew to Australia.

During the hundreds of trips that we took together, we walked five, or ten, or fifteen miles a day in cities as well as in wilderness locations. When we weren't on the road, we took our daily walks on trails in Northern Virginia.

Barbara always wore a pedometer. "It doesn't count if you don't measure it."

We auditioned associates everywhere we went and persuaded our picks to handle our inquires in their regions. Wherever we wanted to personally investigate, we had a local, licensed, associate with us. They knew the territory and had good contacts.

Our most remarkable trip was to Norway. We sailed on a coastal express ship and hit a couple dozen ports of call, in fjords, up to near Russia and back down to Bergen. At each stop we disembarked and walked around the towns and villages.

Barbara had studied Norwegian for months before we went. She said it was the most difficult language she had ever learned. Her problem was that most of the Norwegians we met spoke English and were not very gregarious. She did get some practice, however.

After the cruise, we went to Oslo for the Christmas holidays. That was the shocking part of the journey.

"You will need to be checked out by closing time," the hotel manager told me on Christmas Eve.

"We are not checking out,' I said. "We are staying here for another week."

"But tomorrow is Christmas."

"That's why we're here."

"So, you have family here. Correct?"

"Incorrect. We have no family here."

"Why would you be here on Christmas if you have no family here?"

"To enjoy your beautiful city."

"But everything will be closed tomorrow. Including this hotel."

"Even though we have reservations, you are closing the hotel?"

"Of course. Everyone who works here will be at home with their families on Christmas."

"Is there another hotel where we can…"

"No. What kind of people would work on Christmas?"

"When we made the reservation, you should have told us."

"Your American travel agent should have told you."

I turned to Barbara. "Perhaps you could explain our situation in Norwegian."

"No. He's made it abundantly clear. They are going to throw us out in the snow on Christmas Eve and let us starve and freeze until Boxing Day."

The manager said, "You truly have nowhere to go?"

"We truly don't," I said.

Barbara said, "We can make our own bed and eat sandwiches if we can find the fixings at a local market."

"No stores are open now, ma'am. But we have a bartender who will be staying here. I think he has some nuts or something to eat."

I said, "Does he speak English, or only Norwegian?"

"He doesn't speak Norwegian, but he does speak English. He's from Malta. That's why he doesn't have family here."

"Excellent," I said. "Please introduce us to our fellow prisoner."

A smile flickered across the manager's face. That was as close as I ever came to making that stern Norwegian laugh.

"The doors must all remain locked," the boss said. "The bartender has a key to one door in case you wish to take a walk."

Thus, on Christmas morning, 1986, we ate pretzels for breakfast with a Maltese bartender in an Oslo hotel.

When the midday twilight finally illuminated the city, a little, the three of us walked through the deserted metropolis in a light snowfall. Not a creature was stirring. No trolleys, no buses, no taxis. No electric lights.

Barbara was the first to hear the singing. She led us to a makeshift church where a dozen other foreigners were huddled, being serenaded by a Christian minister playing a guitar. She did not speak English.

Barbara translated for the congregation. Our holy hostess offered the starving supplicants reindeer steaks, a traditional Christmas meal in Norway.

And to make it even more special, she told us these would be the last reindeer steaks for thousands of years, due to the nuclear power plant disaster at Chernobyl eight months earlier.

The cloud of radiated materials had drifted over the Nordic countries and contaminated the acorns on which the reindeer feed, so only those pre-Chernobyl steaks would be edible.

Perhaps due to the rarity of the repast, God's representative required us all to sing for our supper, not any Christmas carols that we knew, but Norwegian hymns we had never heard before.

With Barbara's patient, persistent help, the hungry herd was finally able to satisfy the strict musical missionary. Starvation is the best sauce for food. Those steaks were delicious.

A dozen years later, we came across a reindeer ranch in New Zealand. The Norwegian owner had migrated there to raise reindeer in a more pleasant climate, prior to Chernobyl. Suddenly, the demand from his homeland, particularly at Christmas time, had made his financial future secure.

---

"Can you hear me, sweetheart?"

"Just barely," said Barbara.

It was afternoon in Sri Lanka, but pre-dawn in Virginia.

I explained. "We were supposed to fly over Baghdad, but the Americans started bombing it, so we diverted to Tashkent. There was a hassle buying jet fuel in Uzbekistan. That's where we were delayed."

I didn't tell her till later that we were close enough to see the bomb blasts in Baghdad as our pilot turned the airliner when the Gulf War began. We could not see the stealth bombers flying in our direction, only their fiery footprints on the ground and the anti-aircraft artillery and rockets trying to find them in the air.

"But you're in Colombo now, right?" she asked.

"Yeah. I knew you'd be worried."

"Of course. You were flying in a war zone. It's all over the news."

When we didn't travel together, it was always stressful. Communications were far more difficult in those days.

After flying me first-class halfway around the world, our client's lawyers in Sri Lanka wanted to make changes in our engagement agreement, which they had had for weeks. I took a lot of notes and faxed them to Barbara from The International Hotel.

She typed and signed the new agreement and faxed it back to me. I made copies for the client's lawyers.

That was cutting edge technology in 1991. And it was expensive.

The next morning, the lawyers were flabbergasted. They had expected me to use snail mail and come back to them in a month or so.

In fact, I was in Sri Lanka for over a month, due to the Gulf War.

As Barbara conducted the investigation in the United States, she and I communicated daily, and I apprised the client firm, and their lawyers.

--------

Later that year, Barbara took a trip without me.

"Trish is moving to Santa Fe. Can you hold down the fort here while I ride with her and her dogs?"

"Sure. You gonna take turns driving?"

"No. I don't think so. I think her Audi is a stick shift."

--------

"Hey, Barbara. Trish wants to talk to you."

"Hello, Trish. I'm all packed for tomorrow. What's up?"

After a long conversation, Barbara hung up the phone. "What a mess. Trish had everything boxed up and ready for her moving van to arrive. But it didn't. Her renter's furniture is supposed to be delivered today, but Trish's stuff is still in the house."

"What's the problem with her moving company?"

"She has had a contract with Bekins for months, but when they didn't show up on time, she called, and they said they don't have a truck available."

"Did they say when they would be there?"

"The first guy she spoke to said they had three days to get there, but that's not what the contract says. It says they must deliver her stuff in Santa Fe in three days."

"You've read the contract?"

"I have."

"Could they store her things locally until they free up a van?"

"Trish suggested that, but Bekins headquarters said they didn't have any small local trucks or storage facilities available."

"What do her renters say?"

"I don't think she has been able to reach them. Three pilots and one of the pilot's wives will be living there. They are expecting the house to be empty today."

"What can we do?" I asked Barbara, thinking there might be some legal remedy for this breach of contract.

"We can rent a moving truck. I can drive it to New Mexico."

"Have you ever driven a big truck before?"

"No. Do they come with an automatic transmission?"

"Some do."

"Where can we get one?"

"Penske Truck Rental is right around the corner, over by Red Lobster."

------

"Trish *would* live on a treelined street," Barbara said from the cab once she stopped the moving truck at Trish's house. "Look back there at all the branches I've knocked down."

"Tree branches aren't a problem, but you have to be careful about overhead clearances. Like overpasses and gas stations for example. Make sure you have enough headroom for this thing. Okay?"

"Okay. I'll be careful."

"Watch me in you mirror and I'll guide you while you back to the door."

Working together, we got the moving truck close to the house, crunching a rain gutter on the garage on route.

The new renters, along with a moving van full of their furniture, and movers to put it into the house, waited while the casual laborers we picked up crammed Trish's belongings into the Penske rental.

Barbara drove it home and parked it on the street outside our condo.

---

"Okay, Barbara, take these headphone transmitters that we use on surveillances so you and Trish can talk to each other."

"Good idea, Harry. I'll be following her, but we might get separated in highway traffic."

"And every time you stop, give me a call."

"Don't worry."

"Sweetheart, you will be driving a truck for your very first time, nearly two thousand miles on major highways, with a heavy load. Of course, I'm gonna worry."

---

"Hello, Mr. Gossett?"

"Yes?"

"The lady in the big yellow truck told me to call you about the gas pump she knocked over."

"What! Was there a fire?"

"No. Gas pumps have an automatic cutoff valve when they get knocked over."

"Is she alright?"

"I reckon. She paid for her gas, but she said you would pay for the damage."

"Hmm."

"You see, I couldn't tell her how much it would cost to put the pump back up."

"No problem. Just give me your name and address and the amount, and I'll mail you a check."

---

"Did the guy from the gas station call you, Harry."

"He did. What happened?"

"You told me to watch out for the overhead clearance at gas stations, so I was looking up. I forgot how long my big monster is, so I brushed against a gas pump a little."

"He said you knocked it over."

"It fell over. But I didn't hit it hard."

"Are you okay?"

"I don't know. Do you know how much gas this thing uses?"

"What did you expect? You're hauling a five-bedroom house."

"And our two-way radios aren't working."

"Oh."

"You know we have to plug them in the cigarette lighter holes?"

"Yeah."

"The Penske truck doesn't have a cigarette lighter plug-in."

"Are you having any trouble following Trish?"

"I've been able to keep her in sight, and of course, she has no problem seeing the huge yellow box behind her."

"How are those big dogs doing?"

"Fine. They seem to be enjoying the ride. Whenever we stop, I walk Ginger and Trish takes Pepper."

---

"How was your day today, trucker?"

"The road around Memphis was so rough I could hear my cargo shifting."

"Is the truck leaning?"

"I don't think so. I'm getting comfortable driving it. We're doing okay."

"You must have put in quite a few miles today, Barbara, since you're calling so late."

"That's not all. We walked Ginger and Pepper around the motel parking lot in the dark. They slipped under a fence and romped around an open field. When they came back to us, we discovered they had been rolling around in manure. Why do dogs do that?"

"Camouflage, I think."

"Camouflage? They looked like two dogs wearing dung overcoats. That wouldn't fool anybody."

"They hunt with their noses. So, any predator who is trying to sniff them out will mistake them for a pile of poop."

"Not anymore. We scrubbed them down in the bathtub. Washed off so much crap it stopped up the drain."

"At least you got a little workout."

"Harry, why didn't you tell me I didn't have to stop at weight stations?"

"You've been stopping at weight stations?"

"Every one of them. And it was most inconvenient for Trish. There was nowhere for her to put her car while I was waiting in line to get my truck weighed."

"You're not driving a commercial vehicle, so I don't think you have to pull into the weight stations."

"I know that now. At the fourth one I visited, they told me."

---

"Where are you now, Baby?"

"Tucumcari, New Mexico."

"Do they still have that big "T" on the mountain that you can see from the highway?"

"I didn't notice. We got here after dark. Trish and I left the dogs in our motel room and ate with a bunch of bikers in the restaurant."

"Some sort of a motorcycle rally?"

"I don't know. The only vehicles other than ours were Harley Davidsons. Your dad would have been proud."

"He would have. As you know, he not only sold Harleys, but he also grew up in New Mexico."

"Have you ever seen the Cadillac Farm, Harry?"

"Only in magazines."

"Me, too. But I wanted to see it in person. I got Trish to follow me off I-40. I didn't tell her where we were going. I wanted to see the look on her face when she saw those ten Cadillacs buried nose deep in the dirt."

"I forgot you took a travel folder with you."

———————

"Happy fourth of July, Harry. We are now in Santa Fe. The end of the road."

"I am so relieved."

"You ever been to Santa Fe?"

"Many times."

"You know how twisty and turny the streets are."

"And I know how big that truck is. Did you hit anything?"

"No indeed. I've gotten so good with the yellow elephant that I whipped it around Santa Fe's narrow streets with no problems."

"I'm impressed."

"Remember I told you the furniture moved around at Memphis?"

"Yeah. Anything broken?"

"I don't know. But I told the guys that Trish got to do the unloading to be careful and open the back doors slowly. Nobody listened to me. They got buried in an avalanche of boxes."

"Anyone hurt?"

"Nah. Trish is feeling sick though. I think it is the altitude."

"How are you feeling?"

"Great! What a beautiful city. Most of the streets have Spanish names. I feel right at home."

"I hope Trish is not helping haul any heavy stuff into her house."

"She should lie down but she insists on following me to Penske's so she can drive me back. I told her I could take a cab. She said, 'This isn't New York City. You can't just flag down a cab.'"

"I'll feel better knowing you're back in a car, even with a nauseous driver."

---

"Good morning, *esposo*. Oh, I forgot the time difference. *Buenas tardes*."

"Well, top o' the morning to you, Barbara. Are you still feeling well?"

"I am, but Trish not so much. She thought pancakes for breakfast would settle her stomach. But she threw up in the parking lot before we even got into the pancake place."

"Let's hope passersby didn't think she was coming out."

"She's feeling a little better now. I think she's gonna be alright."

"You want to stay a few days?"

"Not now that I've met the neighborhood representative."

"Welcome wagon?"

"No. A drunk woman in a two-piece bathing suit staggered up to the door and said, 'I'm one of your neighbors. Are you two a couple?' She was quite threatening."

"What did you say?"

"I said, 'I am leaving tomorrow to fly back to my husband in Virginia.' Her entire body relaxed. I thought she was going to melt into an alcoholic puddle on the porch."

---

Our friend Marv wrote a textbook and conducted seminars for state CPA societies on Fraud Auditing Techniques, as a representative of the American Institute of Certified Public Accountants.

Throughout the 1990s he hired me to do the same, using his textbook.

Marv and I took turns winning the best instructor award each year. The CPAs rate their instructors.

I took Barbara with me the very first time. She explained the relevant legal issues to the accountants. However, she was worse than bored, she was intimidated, by the math I talked about during the bulk of the days.

"They don't laugh at the jokes, Harry. They don't even blink their eyes."

"They scored high marks on the final exam. That's all I care about."

She declined to ever attend another CPA seminar, so I took five or ten week-long trips each year without her.

---

"I want to learn to fly an airplane, Harry."

"Why?"

"Do I need a reason?"

"It's an expensive hobby. But if we had a business purpose it would be deductible as a business expense."

"I thought you might say that. Terry tells me that the U.S. Marshal's Service is going to stop providing marshals to the federal courthouses. They are going to hire private security guards."

Terry was a dear friend and a private investigator who had been an inspector in the Marshal's Service.

I said, "So, if my security company bids on the contracts for the federal courthouses in Virginia, we can fly around and conduct inspections whenever we want to. Right?"

"Right. But first, I need to learn how to fly. I'm already a certified boat captain."

"The air is less forgiving than the water. You can't break the low altitude record, sweetheart, you can only tie it."

Thus, we started taking flying lessons. We didn't win any of the contracts, and we didn't deduct any of the costs, but we did have a lot of fun.

Fortunately for Barbara, the Federal Aviation Administration had started to allow applicants to use pocket calculators during the written exams.

She had no problem understanding the airplane, regulations, weather, or traffic patterns. But in those pre-GPS days, it was the math required to do the navigation that she needed help with. Plotting a course on a paper map involved both magnetic declination and magnetic deviation.

Her little pocket calculator made it possible for my non-numerate spouse to pass the test.

Barbara became a proud member of The Ninety-Nines, an International Organization of Women Pilots.

Recently, a friend recalled hearing a dedication on National Public Radio back in 1998: "From Barbara to Harry." The song was "You Are the Wind Beneath My Wings."

Our friend had no idea Barbara had ever piloted an aircraft.

# CHAPTER TWENTY-FOUR
## *Twenty-first Century Travel*

"What do you think, Barbara, should we cancel our trip to Portugal?"

"I can take my pocket calculator in case the navigator needs my help."

Her silly response put the problem in prospective.

As the Gregorian calendar marched relentlessly toward the end of the 20th century, the world was holding its breath.

Allegedly all computers used programs written in the 1960s which identified the years with two-digit numbers. What would happen when the year became a double zero? Would all the computers in the world crash?

If so, would the electric power grid and water systems stop? Would telephones and radios fall silent? Would airplanes fall out of the sky?

This potential disaster was called the "Century Date Change" or the "Faulty Date Logic" or the "Millennium Bug," but "Y2K" became the universal abbreviation for the problem. That stood for the "Year 2,000."

Perception is reality and Y2K had everyone in the civilized world frightened because our trusted experts were panicked. Program patches were distributed but no one was confident they would prevent world-wide havoc.

Barbara and I decided that pilots, like my dad, had flown airplanes before there were computers. And airlines would not be putting their planes up if a catastrophe was likely.

So, we took off to Lisbon. From there we drove to Evora, a fabulous place for Barbara and me to spend a vacation.

It's a charming town with walkable cobbled streets lined with traditional painted houses and sur-rounded by an ancient city wall, first erected by the Romans, after they took the hilltop away from the Celts, two generations before Christ was born.

The Romans also built a monumental Corinthian temple in the historic center of the city.

Additional structures and relics were left by over a century of Visigoth rule, 350 years of Moorish domination, and more than 800 years of various Christian kings.

As was our custom, we took day trips to points of interest outside our base. For example, we visited Almendres Cromlech, a megalithic complex in the Alentejo, which consists of several cromlechs and menhir stones.

One afternoon while Barbara was out shopping for groceries, I thought a miracle had happened. As soon as she entered our apartment, I shared it with her. "I'm starting to catch on to this Portuguese language."

"Really?"

"I have been watching the news. And suddenly I realized I could understand it. I can tell you about every story they've reported."

Barbara tried not to laugh. "Sweetheart, you're watching the Spanish channel."

---

Finally, the moment of truth arrived. We listened to the countdown to Y2K on the plaza in Evora where we had been eating street food, enjoying music, watching dancers, and listening to political speeches.

Alas, nothing bad happened.

However, chaos characterized our return flight.

To reduce the number of passengers who would have to be flown back to Portugal if they were not allowed to enter the United States, we were required to go through U.S. Customs and Immigration checks at the Lisbon Airport.

We boarded our plane and it taxied out to the runway.

Then the captain announced that our airline had filed for bankruptcy, and he was not sure he was authorized to fly us home. He guessed it would take considerable time to find out what he was supposed to do, so he was going to take us back to the terminal where we could relax while our future was being ironed out.

We went through Portuguese Customs and Immigration (Alfândega e Imigração) to get back into the building.

Our flight was called again immediately after Barbara and I had ordered lunch, but before it had been served. We paid for it and went back through U.S. Customs and Immigration.

Once more out on the runway, the pilot announced that his fuel gauges were not working. The fuel tanks had just been topped off, but he was not allowed to take off with faulty fuel gauges. No replacements were available in Lisbon, but he hoped the airline could fly in fuel gauges from some nearby European airport. In the meantime, he was taking us back to the terminal.

This time, after we cleared Alfândega e Imigração, we got to eat our lunch before the announcement sent us back through U.S. Customs and Immigration and onto the plane for our long ride home.

Out on the runway, a very disappointed captain informed us that our cockpit crew had been on duty too many hours for them to start a transatlantic flight. Apparently, they had been hoping no one would notice. "We are just as disappointed as you are ladies and gentlemen. We all live in New York."

Back to the terminal and back through Alfândega e Imigração.

The bar was doing a booming business, while we waited for a fresh flight crew to be assembled.

Once more unto the breach, Barbara and I were first in line at U.S. Customs and Immigration. And the first to be separated and taken aside for confrontational interviews.

Looking at my passport in his hand, the official said, "You have flown in and out of Lisbon Airport three times already today. And now you are outbound, again. You know what that tells us?"

"That my airline went bankrupt?"

"No. This is the profile of a drug smuggler."

"Personally, I don't mind a strip search, but my wife is gonna have a heart attack."

A man rushed in and whispered to my interrogator, who handed me my passport and said, "You're good to go."

I found Barbara and we took our place at the end of the line.

A security officer half my age and half my size was apparently feeling empowered. And I was in a grumpy mood.

I was wearing baggy Canadian Army pants which had a metal ring on the waistband for hanging. It triggered the magnetometer.

"You must remove your belt," said the security man.

I took it off and handed it to Barbara, who had already gone through.

"Hold your arms out to the side," he said.

I held out one arm because I was holding up my pants with the other hand.

"Both arms!" he barked."

"If I hold both my arms out, these pants will hit the floor."

"That was not a request. It was a demand!"

Surrounding passengers were starting to watch the show.

I said, "May I speak with your supervisor?"

He indicated a woman a few rows away. "She's busy. Now get those arms out!"

"Okay, tough guy, here you go." I let go of my pants and they crumped around my feet. As it happened, I was wearing black bikini jockey shorts.

He gasped, as did several spectators.

"Are you happy now?" I shouted. "I told you my pants would fall off if I obeyed your ridiculous order. But no! You insisted."

He was looking all around at the witnesses. "Please, sir, pull up your pants."

"How can I? You have me stuck in this both-arms-out position."

He got down on one knee and reached for my pants a time or two but didn't take hold of them. "Please, sir, put your arms down and pull up your pants."

Suddenly the terminal was vibrated by a blood-curdling scream. I recognized Barbara's voice.

Anyone who hadn't been watching before was watching now.

The security supervisor came running, saw her subordinate kneeling before a man with his pants down, did a flying flip turn, and her sneakers screeched on the tiled floor as she ran away.

"I'm begging you, sir," said the lad at my feet.

Having made my point, I pulled up my pants and joined Barbara. While threading my belt through the loops, I said, "Your timing was impeccable. That scream raised the comedy to the next level."

She said, "I wasn't kidding."

"Oh?"

"I looked around and there was my husband half naked standing like that statue of Christ the Redeemer in Rio."

"I know you hate embarrassment."

"Sometimes you are one."

"We will probably have to deal with my little side show again when we get to New York. I might even be arrested for embarrassing the little fascist."

I couldn't have been more wrong. When we finally landed at JFK, the uniformed officials were posted along our route through the terminal, saying, "Get you luggage and get out of here. Everybody in the green line. Go. Go."

I asked one of them, "Don't you want to see my passport?"

"After what you people have been through, we don't want to delay you in the slightest. Just go."

A dozen years later I told this story about dropping my pants in Lisbon to our Aspen friends during one of our annual get togethers. We were having dinner in a private room at a restaurant in Massachusetts.

Several of our colleagues refused to believe I would have been wearing bikini underwear, and thus suggested I had invented, or at least enhanced, the story.

Barbara said, "We're not in public here, Harry. We're among old friends. Show them."

"You want me to drop my slacks?"

"Yes. It annoys me whenever anyone suggests you are not telling the truth."

"Okay." I stood up, removed my blazer, and unbuckled my belt. I pulled up the front of my shirt and lowered my trousers.

At that moment, a young waiter walked into our room—full of people older than his parents. He took one look at me, gulped audibly, said, "Oh, my God," and fled in a gale of laughter.

———————

Another trip that stands out in my mind was a month in China with professors from George Washington University.

"I know they seem to speak a different dialect of Chinese in every city we have visited, Barbara, but I am still amazed at how few words you are picking up and using."

"It's a tonal language, Harry. The same word can mean *mother* or *horse*, depending on your tone of voice."

"But you have an ear for those things. I remember when you prosecuted Chinese drug smugglers."

"So, you should remember that each of them spoke a different dialect. There are more than a dozen Chinese languages."

"Aren't they pretty close?"

"They are about as similar as German and English."

"And you didn't study any of those Chinese languages before this trip."

"There's the major impediment, my darling. I first learn to read a language before I learn to speak it. All the languages I am familiar with are written in the Roman alphabet. I can't read Chinese."

"I'm ashamed that we have been married for thirty years and I didn't know that."

"I have the same problem with Arabic. I can't read it."

# CHAPTER TWENTY-FIVE
## *Preparations for the End*

"It's high time we wrote our wills, Harry."

"Are you feeling okay?"

"I'm feeling fine."

"So am I. Why should we waste our time writing our Last Will and Testament?"

"Because I'm going to be fifty-six next month. My daddy had his annual physical and was declared healthy the day before his fatal heart attack. He was fifty-six."

"Okay. So, fifty-six is the magic number, eh?"

"I'm a lot like my daddy."

"If it makes you feel better, I'll do it. Let's work on our wills together, because one of us is probably going to survive the other."

"In that case, the surviving spouse gets everything. You already know I want my goddaughter Cheryl to get my jewelry. I don't think you will want to wear any of it. We need wills in case we die at the same time."

"Like a plane crash or car wreck?"

"Exactly."

Barbara didn't die when she was fifty-six, but the subject came up again seventeen years later.

"Time for us to update our wills, Harry."

"Good idea. I don't even remember what I wrote last time."

"My mother, and her mother, both died when they were seventy-three. I'll be seventy-three in September."

"So, once again you're thinking about dying?"

"Don't you want me to know what to do with your body if you die first?"

"Surprise me."

Thus, we updated our wills. I was reminded that Barbara did not want a funeral or a celebration of life. She wanted her friends to remember her as she was when they did things together.

Seventy-three came and went without incident, but we made a deal. We would turn in all our professional licenses when Barbara turned eighty. When we stopped working, we could enjoy our remaining years with each other, uninhibited by the pressures of business.

We kept our promise.

Barbara did not hang up her sense of humor when we retired. For example:

While shopping for groceries, my wife encountered a friend from her Spanish book club. They stopped to chat, in Spanish.

An English-speaking woman walked up to them and spoke very slowly and clearly so they could understand. "Excuse me. Would one of you ladies like to clean my house?"

My clever spouse smiled broadly and said, "What a co-incidence! We were just wondering the same thing about you."

The woman wilted and slithered away.

I said, "She had good intentions, Barbara."

"So did I. It was a teaching moment."

---

Barbara even allowed herself to be interviewed by Lisa Zornberg, a woman who had also served as an Assistant United States Attorney in the Southern District of New York, starting twenty-seven years after my wife did. In fact, Ms. Zornberg worked her way up to Chief of the Criminal Division. And she was writing about the women who served as AUSAs in the SDNY.

---

When the Covid-19 pandemic began, Barbara and I took it seriously.

We took our daily walks in the private park belonging to our condominium. We were usually the only ones there.

Once a week we went grocery shopping at stores which were serious about requiring masks and social distancing. Other than that, we were locked down at home.

With paper plates and plastic utensils, we had picnics in each of the seven rooms in our large apartment. We never ate in the bathrooms. Twice we camped out in our tent on the balcony, with a little campfire in our hibachi.

My beautiful wife, Barbara Rowan was far more interested in her heritage than I was in mine. She persuaded me to send in saliva to 23 and Me for a DNA test, when she submitted hers.

On the morning of October 29, 2020, we took our temperatures as we had been doing every morning and evening for over six months. For the first time, we were both running high—really high! 104 degrees!

We rushed to Kaiser Permanente for Covid-19 tests, which we were given immediately.

We both tested positive and were sent in separate ambulances to the Covid ICU at the Virginia Hospital Center where we were both placed on ventilators in individual rooms.

Two days later, she was dead.

# CHAPTER TWENTY-SIX

# *Epilogue*

Nine days after Barbara died, I was sent home in an ambulance, and wheeled to our apartment on a gurney.

There were ten tanks of oxygen in my living room, an oxygen generator, and a mile of hose. I spent two weeks on oxygen, barely able to travel from room to room on a walker. I didn't get out of my hospital gown for three weeks.

One of the items I found in the mountain of mail at our home was a test kit from *23 and Me*. The cover letter said Barbara had submitted insufficient saliva and asked that she try again. Too late for that.

They found more than 99% of my DNA came from the Island of Britain and the other faction of one percent may have come from Norway or Ireland.

Barbara Rowan's DNA would have been much more interesting. From family lore and records research, we had learned that her eight great-grand-parents were:

> One African American
>
> Two Cubans
>
> Two German Jews
>
> Two Jamaicans
>
> One Native American

So, what did that make her? Black, of course. Any non-white was considered "colored" in the southern states, like Virginia where her maternal grandmother came from, and where we lived for forty-three years.

I had observed her being targeted by constant cultural cuts which White people think appropriate or don't notice. She was able to rise above racist remarks and slights far more good-naturedly than I would have. And she insisted that I stay out of the struggle.

In her computer I found a file addressed to me. It included this biographical sketch and said I could share it with anyone.

# MY BEAUTIFUL LIFE

*By Barbara Rowan*

To enhance objectivity (and not because I think I'm royal) I address myself in the third person here.

Barbara Ann Rowan was born at Sloan Pavilion of Columbia Presbyterian Hospital in New York City on September 6, 1938, to Clara Obey Rowan and Norman Barrington Rowan.

Norman was born on November 14, 1906, at Port Antonio, Jamaica, British West Indies. His father, Wellesley George Rowan, and his mother Eugenia Burke of Cuba, separated, leaving Norman to be cared for by his Rowan family Aunts. He came to New York in 1921 to live with his Aunt Francis Allen Rowan, and attend school. He graduated from New York's DeWitt Clinton High School and City College 1929 with a degree in accounting.

Clara was born in Philadelphia, PA in 1909 to Mary Wood (of King William Virginia). She was adopted, almost immediately after birth by Mary and Lee Obey, also former Virginians, and spent her early years surrounded by the Obey family which soon included two brothers, Andrew Lee and Charles. Clara graduated from Girls High School, Philadelphia and then came to New York to join her birth mother Mary Wood Brown.

Norman and Clara met in the Caribbean social world of the New York Harlem YMCA where they made life-long friends. They married on January 19, 1933.

Norman became a US Citizen on July 5, 1939. He was employed as an Accountant by the prestigious firms of A.W. Tucker and later Lucas and Tucker from 1933-1938, followed by the State of New York, Department of Labor, while also maintaining a private practice on 125th Street, where he was aided by Clara as his assistant and secretary. He died in 1963.

Barbara was their only child. She grew up nurtured and surrounded by the comprehensive West Indian community of friends and family, as well as Virginia and Pennsylvania relatives.

Her Paternal Grandfather, Wellesley George Rowan, after spending many years travelling in the Caribbean and South America, had come to live in New York, married Gladys Finlayson and produced four daughters who were added to the group. The four girls and Barbara so closely resembled each other that they were often mistaken for one another in their social circles. All the girls graduated from college and went on to satisfying careers.

Norman, Clara, and Barbara moved to 310 Convent Avenue in 1940 and continued to live in that same apartment until Barbara married in 1972. They were sometimes joined in residence by Aunt Francis and Clara's mother, Mary Wood Brown. Their home was the stopping off point for many Jamaicans on route to schools in Canada and the UK.

Frequent summers were spent visiting the Wood relatives in Dahlgren, Virginia, and Washington DC, as well as at a farm shared by Mary with the Richardson family in Roxbury, New York.

Barbara attended New York City Schools until third grade, when, with the help of Edward Bernath, then Principal of PS 186, and his wife Kathleen, she was accepted into The Dalton School fourth grade class of 1949. She attended Dalton through High School, graduating in 1956. Barnard College was the next stop. She graduated in 1960 with a degree in Spanish, having also completed the Junior Year in Spain program at the University of Madrid.

Barbara then started work as an interpreter in the Family Court System of New York. She added Italian and some other languages to her portfolio and began work on a master's program in Brazilian Area Studies at NYU. She did not complete that master's program.

She subsequently worked as a Foreign Trademark Coordinator for Richardson-Merrell, Inc., while attending law school in the NYU Evening Law School program beginning in 1964. She graduated in 1968 and was admitted to the New York Bar on her first try.

Barbara worked for South Bronx Legal Services, then joined an NYU classmate to open a legal practice in Greenwich Village.

A Federal legal case she prosecuted on behalf of an NYU Professor client brought her to the attention of a Federal District Judge who suggested she apply to be an Assistant United States Attorney (AUSA) in the Southern District of New York. She did so and was hired in1970 to join the Criminal Division as one of the first Black Women in the office. She remained in the office, happily prosecuting federal drug cases for both the Office of Drug Abuse Law Enforcement and fraud cases until 1974 when she returned to law practice in lower Manhattan, joining two wonderful colleagues and dear friends: Elliot Taikeff and Stuart Holtzman.

Sometime in 1971, while acting as the criminal intake AUSA, Barbara apparently caught the attention of Harold Gossett, an FBI Special Agent newly arrived in New York. They were introduced, he was interested, but Barbara tried to introduce him to a good friend of hers, thinking they would be a better match. It was a bad guess.

As a former Marine, Harry would not admit defeat, so they were married on January 19, 1972, by Judge Justine Wise Polier, who was one of those kind Family Court Judges who had recommended Barbara to NYU Law School.

What a wonderful marriage we have had. I cannot imagine a better life partner: happy and laughing, smart, curious, patient, and loving, adventurous travel companion, trustworthy and kind. What else can I say? There is so much more.

Harold W. Gossett II was born in Joplin, Missouri on October 19, 1942, to Harold W. Gossett and Vera Evelyn Smith Gossett. Their families have long roots in North Carolina, New Mexico, and Missouri. He attended High School in Joplin. He was a paper boy, a carpenter's helper, loaded hay and held many other jobs. He played High School Football while working, supporting himself, from age 15 onward, and attending school. He enlisted in the United States Marine Corps in 1959.

He says he was blessed or cursed by peace and did not remain in the Corps, but "Once a Marine, Always a Marine."

Working as a volunteer Deputy Sheriff, Harry met two FBI agents who recruited him to work for the FBI Security Patrol on night shifts while attending college in the daytime, first at Kansas City Junior College, then the University of Missouri at Kansas City and finally at the University of Puerto Rico, where classes were taught in Spanish, his now second language. He graduated from UPR with a B.A. in Social Psychology, later receiving his M.A. in Crimes in Commerce from the George Washington University.

Harry entered FBI Special Agent Training at Quantico, Virginia in 1968 and was sworn in as a Special Agent later that year. He was assigned to field offices in Miami, Florida; New York, New York and

Washington, DC, where he was a supervisor. Before he left the FBI in 1983, he had worked undercover in more than 50 cases, managed the criminal informant programs in New York and Washington and trained many agents in investigation of international frauds, corruption of corporate and public officials, financial crimes against businesses and others.

In 1977, Harry and Barbara were invited to join the Korean Influence Investigation Staff of the House Committee on Standards of Official Conduct in the 95th Congress. The Bureau agreed to lend Harry to the Staff, and they left New York for Washington DC taking Barbara's mother and their three Yorkshire Terriers along for their new lives in the developing Prince William County, Virginia.

Clara died in Virginia in 1982.

Harry returned to the Bureau in 1979 as a Supervisory Special Agent, in the Washington Field Office and Barbara was hired as an Assistant Director of the Federal Trade Commission in the Bureau of Consumer Protection.

She left the FTC to return to private practice, this time in Alexandria VA.

By 1980 she saw a different path and founded ROWAN ASSOCIATES, an Investigative Consulting firm, working for law firms and corporate lawyers.

In 1983 Harry joined Barbara and amazingly they worked together for 35 years, until they retired and closed the business in 2018.

During that time, Harry also conducted seminars for the American Institute of Certified Public Accountants for ten years, teaching fraud auditing techniques.

He also took off for 18 months to work for the United States House of Representatives Committee on Government Reform and Oversight as the sole Democratic investigator.

Harry, always active, now writes novels and Barbara doesn't even answer the telephone unless she can identify the name or number of the caller.

They have lived a good life: Travelled much for business and pleasure, enjoyed mental exercise in their business activities and particularly enjoyed the company of one another. Barbara is happy she did not give Harry away.

---

Struggling from disease and depression I tried to notify everyone I could think of who needed to know Barbara was dead. Their number was enormous. And I missed quite a few.

For a year I received a telephone call for Barbara nearly every day from a friend who had not been informed.

I felt like I was stabbing them in the heart. Many broke up on the phone and had to call back for details.

One posted the following on Facebook and later gave her permission for me to publish it here.

When I was a young lawyer, a couple of years out of law school, I was hired by the House of Representatives Committee on Standards of Official Conduct, to staff the investigation of allegations of improper influence by the government of South Korea. I felt way in over my head, a sense that was heightened one day, very early in my tenure, when two new staff members arrived. They were Barbara Rowan, former Assistant U.S. Attorney in the Southern District of New York, and her husband, Harry Gossett, an FBI agent.

To say that I was intimidated by this couple is an understatement. I was awestruck. They came from Manhattan! She had been a Federal prosecutor and he an investigator for the most prestigious U.S. Attorney's office in the country! They knew what they were doing! I was pretty sure that I did not, and I was just waiting to be found out.

Within a short time, Barbara and I were assigned to share an office with one other attorney (another S.D.N.Y. alum) and a secretary. I was unhappy about this, because (1) at my last job, I had my own cubicle, and (2) did I mention I was intimidated by her? Also by our other attorney office-mate, Tom Fortuin, who wore his self-confidence like one of his beautifully-fitted suits.

Reluctance to share an office with these two was one of many ways in which I was stupid in those days, but I quickly started to get smarter. Sometimes Tom and Barbara told me how to do things, but mostly I just absorbed what they were doing. I got to watch and hear them every day, talking to witnesses and their lawyers, discussing the investigation, dictating documents to our secretary (this was something you could do, in those days), preparing for depositions, planning hearings. From Barbara, in particular, who had been among the first Black female prosecutors in the Southern District, I learned how a tone of voice could command respect. I learned how to initiate contact with a prospective witness ("This is Miss Rowan," was how she began her phone calls), and how to respond to counsel (so many!) who were acting like jerks (icy politeness, and an explanation of the Committee's subpoena power). I learned that, if you do your job, you can know that the guy on the other side, who seems so sure of his position, is bluffing. He doesn't know more than you do; he probably knows considerably less.

I also learned humility. One day, a young woman attorney (even younger than me!) came to seek advice on some work she was doing for another committee that related to our investigation. I brushed her off. As she left the office, I heard Barbara say softly, to no one in particular, "How soon they forget." I felt ashamed of myself. Every young lawyer I ever helped after that has Barbara to thank.

In my long career, I was privileged to work with two ambassadors, one former Cabinet Secretary, five Supreme Court clerks, and many other highly talented and skilled attorneys. I learned a lot from all of them, but no one taught me more than Barbara Rowan, or anything more important. There were not many experienced women lawyers to serve as role models when I was just starting out. I was incredibly lucky to have her as mine.

Two days ago, I received an e-mail from Harry, letting me know that Barbara died of COVID on Halloween. He was also treated in the ICU and is still recovering.

As I wrote back to Harry at once, I am devastated by this news. It is not right, it is not fair. I am so angry and so sad. I am mad at people who don't take this virus seriously, who don't wear masks and hold large indoor gatherings. I am mad about the whole state of affairs that has led to the United States having the highest rate of infection in the developed world.

But most of all, I am angry at myself. Over the last few months, as I've been spending so much time alone, I've been thinking a lot about the past and the people who've touched and enriched my life. I thought of Tom Fortuin, who died of AIDS in the early nineties. It was Barbara who let me know this. I thought about Barbara, and I thought I should let her know how much she meant to me. But I didn't.

I hope this experience makes me better. I'm sure I could improve my own pandemic protocols, but mostly I hope to get better at being a friend. Not a Facebook friend, a real friend. There are one or two other people who may not know how much they made my life better. I need to get in touch, offline.

In the meantime, please wear your mask.

---

I was quite surprised to learn that Martha was intimidated by Barbara, and me! She was the brightest young lawyer I have ever had the privilege to work with. We were pitted against the Korean Central Intelligence Agency, a few corrupt members of Congress, and a herd of experienced lawyers. It was Martha who got the only confession under oath from one of our targets.

---

One of the callers I had to tell that Barbara was permanently unavailable was Lisa Zornberg, who called with some follow-up question to her interview four months earlier.

She published the following:

**Author's note**: I had the great fortune of interviewing Barbara Rowan on July 14, 2020. I'd reached out to her as part of a historical project I'm working on about the pioneering female AUSAs of SDNY, and to better understand how SDNY's doors truly and irrevocably opened to women lawyers in the 1970s.

265

Barbara Rowan was one such pioneer. I called her out of the blue and we spent a marvelous, few hours speaking. Barbara willingly shared with me her time and reflections. She even acceded to my requests (my begging, really) to send me some old photographs. After learning of her untimely death due to COVID-19, I've drafted this piece from the notes of our interview and my follow-up research to share with the SDNY community. I hope she would have approved.

Lisa Zornberg

The year was 1971 and Barbara Rowan was searching for a casefile. A case had been reassigned to her and she couldn't find the file anywhere. So at a Criminal Division meeting – which at the time consisted of a roomful of men and just two women – Barbara asked her fellow AUSAs whether they'd mind if she looked through their file drawers. One AUSA quipped, "Oh Barbara, you can come look in my drawers any time." To which she shot back: "Oh Peter, I've already looked in your drawers and found them to be empty." The room exploded with uproarious laughter.

Barbara was always witty and quick-tongued. Perhaps that explains her talent for languages. She spoke multiple languages and, after graduating from Barnard College, Barbara worked in the New York family courts as a professional interpreter of Italian and Spanish. In the course of her life, she was many things, a linguist among them. She was also the first black woman ever sworn in an Assistant United States Attorney in the Southern District of New York. And she was the third woman ever to serve in the Criminal

Division — after Florence Perlow Shientag (1943) and Shirah Neiman (September 1970).

The *New York Times* did not report the event of Barbara Rowan's swearing in. To her male colleagues, there were no great ripples upon her arrival. But it mattered a great deal in Harlem. To the *New York Amsterdam News* — a leading black newspaper of the time, based in Harlem, where Barbara grew up — it was front page news. The paper carried this headline on February 13, 1971:

# Women's Lib: Hospital Director; Asst. U. S. Attorney
(Stories in Columns 4, 3, 6 and 8)

The paper ran two lead stories under that headline: one about the Harlem woman who was the first black woman ever to serve as head of a major municipal hospital, and the other about Barbara Rowan's appointment as an AUSA.

"Miss Rowan," a 32-year old New York City native, "is the first black woman to be named to the New York post and only one of two females in the Criminal Division," the article read. The news of her appointment spread well beyond Harlem, in fact — all the way to Jamaica, her father's birthplace, where the local press picked it up, too. I dare ask, how many AUSAs can say their appointment was reported in the foreign press?

When I interviewed Barbara in July 2020, I asked her if – looking back – she felt herself a part of the "women's lib" movement of the 1970s. Not really, was her answer. After her father had died at a young age, the responsibility of being the breadwinner fell to Barbara.[1] "I needed a career that would earn money to support my family." The women's rights movement seemed remote to her, less urgent, and less inviting to a black woman.

---

1 *The Amsterdam News* article erroneously reported that Barbara's father, Norman Rowan, was still alive at the time of her swearing in. When I called that to Barbara's attention, she chuckled, emailing "I guess some fake news is always available. My dear dad died in 1963, but I guess his spirit lived on in our home or at least in the *Amsterdam News.*"

# First Black Woman U.S. Asst. Attorney

**(Photo on Page 23)**

The federal Attorney General's Office has announced the appointment of Miss Barbara Ann Rowan as U.S. Assistant Attorney in the Southern District of New York State.

Miss Rowan is the first black woman to be named to the New York post and only one of two females stationed in the Criminal Division.

The announcement was made by Whitney North Seymour, Jr. (shown here at the swearing-in ceremony), U. S. Attorney of the District, which covers the 2nd Federal Circuit area. Her duties incorporate the prosecution of violators of the Federal Criminal Law.

### Native New Yorker

A 32-year-old native of New York City, Atty. Rowan is a graduate of New York University School of Law and a member of the New York Bar Assn. Her legal education began at Barnard College and she also holds a Certificate of Language and Literature from the University of Madrid, Spain.

Before serving with the Community Action for Legal Services, an organization offering legal services to the poor, she performed as Trademark Coordinator for the Richardson-Merrel Inc. company and as an interpreter of Spanish and Italian in the Family Court. She also devoted six years to summer work in several New York hospitals.

Miss Rowan leaves a stint in private practice to accept the federal post and is a member of the National Conference of Black Lawyers and the National Bar Association, another black attorneys' group.

An accomplished swimmer and dancer, Miss Rowan resides in Harlem with her father, Norman B. Rowan, a longtime Harlem accountant and her mother, Clara. Other legal-minded close relatives include two lawyers and a judge in the Caribbean area.

269

She had started a master's degree program in Brazilian studies and took and passed the exam for the State Department, figuring a career path in diplomacy would make good use of her language skills. But when she interviewed with the State Department, the gentleman told her flatly: "You know we don't hire women." Somehow, that was a perfectly acceptable thing to say in the 1960s. And so Barbara left the master's program and enrolled instead at NYU Law School. She took law school classes by night and worked full time by day.

After graduating in 1968, Barbara and an NYU classmate — a Jewish man who was her friend — together hung out their own shingle in Greenwich Village, on 9th Street. They operated a two-person shop handling whatever legal cases came in. Going the "Big Law" route did not seem to be an option. "I did not think a New York law firm would hire me, and frankly did not want to try to fit the mold that such employment would require," Barbara recalled.

It was Barbara's excellent handling of a case before Southern District Judge Morris Lasker that ultimately led to her AUSA appointment. The case was an employment dispute. Barbara represented the plaintiff, an army colonel who was resident scholar on NYU's faculty. The defendant was NYU, her alma mater, and NYU wanted her client gone from the faculty. Following a hearing, Judge Lasker ruled for the plaintiff (the colonel could stay) and then said,

"Ms. Rowan, can I speak to you at sidebar?" From the bench, Judge Lasker then asked her if she would be interested in going to the U.S. Attorney's Office. The judge recognized talent when he saw it. She said "yes."

Soon after, Barbara got a call from Silvio Mollo, the First Assistant. He was not exactly encouraging, but it could have gone worse. "We're all guys here and we swear a lot," he said. "I understand," she answered. She applied and was hired by U.S. Attorney Mike Seymour.

(**Left**) Barbara Rowan's sworn in by U.S. Attorney in, February 1971. sworn in by U.S. Attorney Whitney North (Mike) Seymour, Jr. (**Right**) Rowan, with her proud mother, at the swearing in. Her father had passed away years earlier and she was the breadwinner of the family.

Barbara Rowan was full of stories and had a gift for delivering them. There was the time she took to trial a 19-defendant prosecution of a Chinese narcotics ring. The courtroom was a zoo. Beyond there being 19 defendants, each one claimed to speak a different dialect of Chinese (as a prong of their defense), so there were also 19 different interpreters. Disagreement broke out at one point among those 19 interpreters about what the Chinese witness on the stand had said. Finally, Ms. Rowan (who didn't speak any Chinese but had an uncanny sense for language) stood up and said, "Your Honor, I think the witness said "shopping bag." "Yes, yes, she's right!" the witness exclaimed.

Then there was the time a narcotics agent called her at home in the middle of the night —at 3:00 a.m. — while she was the AUSA on duty. The agent was of Irish decent, and when she picked up the telephone receiver and introduced herself as AUSA Rowan, he told her what a pleasure it was that a "nice Irish girl" held such an important job. The urgent question of the moment was whether the agent should shoot the dog he found guarding a drug stash. "Good Lord, no, please don't shoot the dog," she told him, "and come to my office in the morning." The next morning, the agent came in looking for the lass with the face of Ireland. At the office labeled "Rowan," he popped his head in and asked the black woman sitting at the desk to "please find this Rowan girl." "I am the Rowan girl," she said.

"Ah Jesus," was the only response he could muster.

They got on just fine.

No one spoke about race. She felt her colleagues and the judges on the bench treated her "normally." There was no discussion of her being the first black woman to serve as an AUSA in the Office. Once though, in an elevator, someone said to Barbara: "Judge Motley, how nice to see you." Barbara mentioned it to Judge Constance Baker Motley. Of course, the two women looked nothing alike. "People think I'm you," she told the judge. Judge Motley's response was: Please be nice.

Barbara Rowan was a great, great trial lawyer, as natural as anybody who ever worked in a courtroom. That's how Rusty Wing — the trial lawyer of trial lawyers — describes and remembers Barbara. To John Siffert, Barbara was his first legal mentor; he interned for her in the summer of 1971, before later becoming an AUSA himself. "I learned so much from her. She was fabulous and she taught me that smart people could have fun practicing law." She left SDNY after three or four years, as was the custom of the day. She owned her own law practice, then went on to run investigations for the U.S. Congress, and ultimately formed and ran for many years an investigations firm with her husband, a former FBI agent.

Barbara Rowan cherished her time at SDNY and adored her colleagues, and they her.

By New Year's Day, 2021, I had recovered sufficiently to start writing this memoir.

Shortly thereafter, I received a call from Benjamin Weiser, a New York Times reporter who usually covered legal matters at the Southern District of New York. He asked for my permission to write a belated New York Times obituary.

I sent him Lisa Zornberg's article and suggested a few people at Barbara's places of employment who could confirm her service to our country and the law.

As he and his team proceeded, I received calls from many whom they interviewed. The Times reporters sought out second and third sources for the facts.

Here's the result of their diligent work:

**THOSE WE'VE LOST**

## Barbara Ann Rowan, Who Spurred Advances for Black Lawyers, Dies at 82

As a Black lawyer she protested a racial slur during a bar association speech after forging a trail as a federal prosecutor in Manhattan. She died of Covid-19.

Barbara Ann Rowan was sworn in as an assistant U.S. attorney in Manhattan by Whitney North Seymour, Jr., the U.S. attorney. She was the first Black woman in that position in the Southern District of New York. Credit...via Rowan family

By Benjamin Weiser

Feb. 18, 2021, 10:53 a.m. ET

*This obituary is part of a series about people who have died in the coronavirus pandemic. Read about others here.*

Barbara Ann Rowan, a transplanted New Yorker practicing law in Virginia, was attending an Alexandria Bar Association event in 1982 when a prominent defense lawyer used a racial slur in delivering an after-dinner speech to more than 100 people.

The lawyer drew a standing ovation when the speech ended, but Ms. Rowan, the only Black attorney present, remained seated, The Washington Post reported.

"It was not a pleasant welcome to the Alexandria Bar," she told The Post. "My goodness, I thought I'd stepped into the last century."

After Ms. Rowan described the incident to Gerald Bruce Lee, a Black lawyer who had encouraged her to attend the event, he said he organized a group of Black attorneys to send a protest letter to the bar. The bar expressed "deep sorrow" over what it called "a mistake by an old man," The Post said. The offending lawyer said he would apologize.

The incident helped spur the formation of a new bar group, the Northern Virginia Black Attorneys Association, said Mr. Lee, who went on to hold state and federal judgeships: "We realized we needed to unite and to support each other and to be our own voice."

Ms. Rowan died at 82 on Oct. 31 at a hospital in Arlington, Va. Her husband, Harold W. Gossett II, a retired F.B.I. agent and her only survivor, said the cause was Covid-19.

Her death was not initially announced because she had not wanted a funeral, said Mr. Gossett, who had also contracted the coronavirus and was hospitalized with his wife. After he recovered, he said, he concluded that she would not have objected to his discussing her life — and her record as a trail blazer.

In 1971, Ms. Rowan, then 32, joined the prestigious U.S. attorney's office for the Southern District of New York, making her the first Black female prosecutor there, according to a front-page article heralding her appointment in The New York Amsterdam News, one of the oldest Black-owned newspapers in the country. The article said she would be one of two women serving in the office's criminal division.

Decades before, Ms. Rowan was an early Black student at the elite Dalton School in Manhattan after it began integrating racially in the 1940s, the school said.

Ms. Rowan was born on Sept. 6, 1938, in Upper Manhattan, the only child of Norman Rowan and Clara (Obey) Rowan. Her father, a naturalized citizen from Jamaica, was an accountant; her mother, from Philadelphia, assisted him in his work, Ms. Rowan wrote in a brief personal history. She was raised in Harlem, and said she grew up "nurtured and surrounded" by a West Indian community of friends and family and other relatives.

She graduated from Dalton in 1956 and from Barnard College in 1960 with a bachelor's degree in Spanish. Also fluent in Italian, she worked as an interpreter in the city's family courts while attending New York University's evening law school program, receiving her law degree in 1968.

Ms. Rowan did stints with South Bronx Legal Services and in private practice, but she soured on criminal defense work partly because she tended to sympathize with her clients' victims, said Geraldine Salvani, a lawyer and friend.

Her hiring by the U.S. attorney's office, then led by Whitney North Seymour Jr., was serendipitous. As she recalled in an interview last summer with Lisa Zornberg — a former criminal division chief who is writing a book on women who served in the office

— a judge, after ruling in Ms. Rowan's favor, asked whether she might want to join the prosecutor's office. She said yes, and received a call from Mr. Seymour's No 2.

"We're all guys here and we swear a lot," he told her.

While records are incomplete, Ms. Zornberg said her research supported Ms. Rowan's distinction as the first Black woman to be appointed prosecutor in the Southern District. Ms. Salvani said, "She was so proud when she got the job."

Ms. Rowan's hiring helped break ground for women generally in the Southern District, especially in its criminal division, where only two or three women had preceded her, said Ms. Zornberg, a partner at Debevoise & Plimpton.

Ms. Rowan in 2006. She had a later career as an investigative consultant, and was known for her high ethical standards in the field. Credit...Courtesy of Matthew J. Maher

Ms. Rowan spent three years prosecuting drug and fraud cases. In courtrooms, she engaged jurors with humor and charm, former colleagues recalled. "She had real jury appeal," said Gary Naftalis, a former supervisor.

Ms. Rowan told Ms. Zornberg, "The experience taught me about myself."

It was during that period that she met Mr. Gossett, who was investigating cases with the office. They married in 1972.

A few years after Ms. Rowan left the Southern District in 1974, she and Mr. Gossett were invited by a former office colleague, John W. Nields Jr., to join the staff of the House ethics committee's "Koreagate" investigation looking into Korean influence-peddling in Congress.

Ms. Rowan subsequently served as an assistant director of the Federal Trade Commission. In 1980, she founded an investigative consulting firm, Rowan Associates, which Mr. Gossett joined after leaving the F.B.I. in 1983.

They worked together for 35 years, retained by law firms, corporations and state and federal agencies, Mr. Gossett said.

Jim Mintz, founder of his own investigative firm and a friend of the couple's, said Ms. Rowan had stood out as someone with enormous integrity in a field where investigators sometimes used ethically challenged methods to gather information.

"She demanded information that she could use in court, and she didn't want to have to be shy about how she got it," Mr. Mintz said.

## Kitty Bennett and Alain Delaquérière contributed research.

Benjamin Weiser is a reporter covering the Manhattan federal courts. He has long covered criminal justice, both as a beat and investigative reporter. Before joining The Times in 1997, he worked at The Washington Post. @BenWeiserNYT

This New York Times obituary caused a torrent of telephone calls from Barbara's friends, some who had known she had passed away and still others who had just learned of her death by reading it.

Many who had been interviewed by the reporters were disappointed that their superlative phrases had not been printed. For example:

"She was a mountain of integrity."

"Barbara was the most alive person I have ever known."

"I am forever grateful that I knew Barbara."

Of course, these are not the sort of comments that belong in an obituary. But I was happy to hear them. I have never met a person who didn't like Barbara Rowan. How much so many folks loved her validated my own feelings.

I jotted down comments from friends who had recently learned of her death:

"Barbara was a perfect person."

"She had an elegant mind."

"Your wife was resilient."

"She never took herself for granted."

"My life has been much richer for having known Barbara."

"I've never had a conversation with Barbara when she didn't make me laugh, and I didn't learn something."

"Barbara was driven, intelligent, complex, and special."

"She was truly a unique, wonderful person."

"Barbara always made everybody laugh."

"What a beautiful mind and spirit!"

"She was a forever friend."

"She changed our lives for the better."

"Her legacy will be remembered by us all."

"Barbara touched me personally and professionally."

"A remarkable person."

"A most beautiful lady, inside and out."

"She brought a level of professionalism to attorneys and allowed no nonsense."

Some praise for my wife rubbed off on me:

"You two were an ideal couple."

"We always called you guys 'the Greenhouse couple.'" (The Greenhouse is the name of our condominium.)

Some comments I didn't have to write down because they came in emails:

I am still in shock about Barbara's passing. There are no words that truly can express my feelings and sympathy. You are in my prayers, thoughts and heart! Goodness the people she (and you) have touched...mentored...bettered their lives in ways you may never truly know! I know I am blessed to have you both in my life!

---

I felt a little sadness today because I still miss her (always will: that's the price we pay for the privilege of knowing and loving special people), but I also smiled at happy memories (like singing together on the bus on a Smithsonian tour). Barbara was one of a kind, and great company. I'm really grateful I had both Barbara and you in my life: you two made my life so much richer than it ever would have been without you.

---

Barbara was the first woman attorney that I met, and the smartest one of all. She was my best friend that I always went to for legal and personal advice. It will take me a while to accept her loss and not being able to see her beautiful face and cheerful smile. Not to mention that wonder voice. My heart is broken.

(This one was not from "Bootsy.")

---

When people said something about how well Barbara and I got along, she often said, "I argue for a living. I certainly wouldn't want to do that at home."

I sometimes think that the only good thing about Racism is that it brings people together. Folks who are discriminated against feel a kinship with one another.

Perhaps you think I should say, "It *forces* people together while prying groups apart." But in my case, it did not compel me to ignore the woman meant for me.

The fact that we expected to be shunned (far more than we ever were) may have made us cling together tighter than other couples, or we might have simply loved one another more than most.

This is the end of this book. But not the end of Barbara's presence in my life. I still love thinking about her. Her voice still speaks to me.